On
ARRAN

Some other books by the author

Kenneth Grahame: An Innocent in the Wild Wood
(Alison & Busby 1994)

The Necessary Goat
(Taranis 1992)

Among many children's books are

A Dog Called You
(Pan 1993)

Merv on the Road
(Pan 1993)

The Blue Moon Day
(Pan 1990)

How's Business
(Pan 1988)

for Liz, Ann, Bridget and Jocy with much love

On
ARRAN

Alison Prince

from Alison, Annie, Lucky and Charlie!

Arran Jan 96

This collection first published 1994
Argyll Publishing
Glendaruel
Argyll PA22 3AE

British Library Cataloguing-in-Publication Data.
A catalogue record for this book is available from the
British Library.

ISBN 1 874640 80 7

Cover photo by Graham Jones
Typeset and origination by Cordfall Ltd, Civic Street
Glasgow G4 9RH
Printed by Martins, Sea View Works, Spittal,
Berwick upon Tweed TD15 1RS

Foreword

Alison Prince was already an established author when she came to live on Arran so I was a little surprised when she approached me and asked if she could write a 'green' column in the Banner. There would be no fee and it must be regular. She readily agreed to both of these conditions and it has been regular, fortnightly, since November 1988.

I saw 'On the Green' first as a feature that would satisfy those among our readership who were green minded. Alison (I think) saw it as a platform for getting recycling off the ground on Arran. Being to mutual advantage is the best thing for any project and on that basis it has worked well.

Recycling, the Green Party, concern for the environment were all at their peak then. These things are not so 'fashionable' now. But 'On the Green' goes on. The reason for this is that the column has developed beyond its original intention. Alison is nothing if not observant and, as she has cast around for topics on the green, on Arran, her eye has alighted on the quirky, the unexpected, often the unsaid. It is all the better for that. Above all it is immensely readable.

This little book is the pick of 'On the Green' and is an easy and enjoyable read, and at the same time it makes you sit up and think.

John Miller, Editor
Arran Banner

Contents

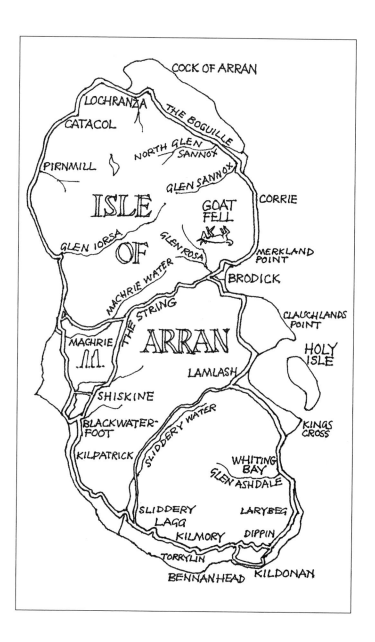

Acknowledgements

The first 'On the Green' Column appeared in the *Arran Banner* on November 5th 1988. It was a suitably explosive date for an outburst of indignation about the Council's refusal to provide Arran with bottle-banks, on the grounds that we were too small a community to make such a project economically viable.

For the next year or so, the column sniped at various ecological targets, and then, with bottle-banks established and the green grumbles teetering on the verge of tedium, it settled into something more like a diary of island life.

I am indebted to John Miller for publishing these pieces without demur, even when they conflicted with his own well-kent moderation, and to the many people who have said they enjoyed them. To my countless friends on Arran this book is dedicated, in the hope that it may provide an echo of that enjoyment.

Alison Prince
Whiting Bay
January 1994

The Largs hum

13 January 1990

SO HERE WE HAVE IT – a naked new-born decade screaming for attention as new-born babies are wont to do. And succeeding pretty well in getting it. 1990 is a natural limelight-hogger. Its antecedents are being raked over with the morbid fascination which is more usually reserved for members of the Royal family, and our expectations of the decade itself reflect the insane confidence which causes people to put Junior's name down for Eton when he is no more than a dose of morning sickness.

Personally, I regard this infant decade with extreme caution. It probably means well, in a mewling and puking sort of way, but just look at its parentage. Did Mr and

15

Mrs Eighties plan a good future for their child? Not them. They enjoyed their ten years of rapacious acquisition and damn the consequences. If the planet groans its way into oblivion they won't be there to see it. Wee Nineties will have just the same attitude unless a very firm line is taken with the growing child to curb its wayward greed. Otherwise the little monster will make the cosmic mess to end them all.

Switzerland of course looks forward to a beautifully clean and tidy decade – as well it might – with bin bags at a compulsory thirty pence a piece as last week's *Banner* reported. Can you imagine the results if we tried to impose such a charge here? People already hurl fridges and old armchairs down the glens for fear of largely illusory coup charges. If rubbish was only lifted in official, paid-for bags, the result would be obvious. Litter dumpers would be out at dead of night in black balaclavas, depositing piles of refuse in places of maximum inconvenience. And there would be enough bonfires to burn a brand new hole in the ozone layer.

Everyone likes the idea of waste stuff being taken away but nobody wants to pay for the service except as a voluntary donation by those who care. (Strangely enough, to judge by the Arran Recycling Company's experience, these are seldom the people who benefit directly from the collection of their unwanted stuff.)

No, the Swiss approach is fundamentally un-British. We would need something more complicated, involving a lot of committee meetings and interim suggestions and head-shaking followed by compromise and all that is implied in the time honoured phrase, "Carry on." A nice comfortable muddle in other words. But then we're not Swiss. Pity really.

Did anyone spot the report in the *Glasgow Herald* on

January 6th of the 'Largs Hum'? People living on the Clyde coast have been kept awake for months now by a low frequency droning noise, particularly noticed by those whose houses are at sea level. This deep rumbling sound has been heard on Arran as well but nobody seems to have any explanation of what causes it.

On many evenings last summer the noise was clearly audible in my own experience, being particularly loud by the sea in Whiting Bay. It's an oddly frightening sound, a heavy rumble which seems to come from the sea itself and it is now beginning to take quite a toll in terms of human distress. People in Largs are getting angry about the constant disturbance of their nights and the emotional stress is in some cases becoming intolerable. One woman admitted, "I walk up and down at night crying."

So what is causing the sound? Nobody will say. Rumour has it that the Admiralty is trying to develop a sonar system which transmits low-frequency signals over hundreds of miles for the detection of submarines. The Ministry of Defence says it can't comment. Too much to hope, one supposes, that they are working on a way to stop submarines from entangling themselves with fishing boats and dragging them to a watery grave? No, there will be some far more arcane purpose than that. There is, after all, a serious danger that international peace may break out. The Hum is probably caused by something quite ordinary – a choir of walruses, say, or a hundred subaquatic cement-mixers. Whatever it is it certainly won't trouble the Swiss.

Doing the little things

27 January 1990

A COUPLE OF WEEKS ago I went to a two day conference in Govan addressed by the American philosopher Noam Chomsky. And what may you ask has this to do with Arran? Quite a lot in a way.

The conference was about 'Self Determination and Power' – in other words, about how we can take control of our own lives. It sounded promising. On an island such as this, the notion of self government is an attractive one. For many people, there has been a kind of 'stepping off the bandwagon' in the very act of coming here. Islanders tend to be people who like the idea of running their own affairs.

Chomsky, who took a brave stand against the US government over the Vietnam War, is well known for his view that people are far more capable of responsible thought and action than officialdom will recognise. He spoke with impressive fluency about the way in which the freedom to organise one's own life is dominated by the simple question of whether one has money or not, and he argued persuasively that society is becoming increasingly repressive. There were nods all round. Kay Carmichael got up when he had finished and asked how all that related to our problems in Scotland and what we should do about it.

"I suggest," said Chomsky, "that you make that the subject of your discussions this afternoon." Neat. You've got to hand it to these philosophers, they know how to get out of a tight spot.

The discussion groups produced huge amounts of hot air. I began to ponder on the feasibility of conference-powered heating schemes for Govan flats. Everyone wanted to change society and nobody knew how to start. Most of the men were for some kind of political solidarity and everyone agreed that you shouldn't pay the Poll Tax. Then a woman said, "I think it's all to do with everyday life. The first time I did anything self-determined was when I managed to confront a teacher at my son's school about the reasons why he was utterly miserable there."

The political theorists looked bored but every one else brightened up. There's something immensely refreshing about practicality. By the end of the conference, two distinct groups had emerged – the Practicals and the Theorists. Me, I'm a Practical, as were almost all the other women. It seemed to us that the only way to make any sort of move towards a more caring society is to start in the small ways which present themselves in everyday reality. By saying what you think rather than keeping quiet for fear of being thought stupid. By defending our kids' right to be themselves rather than conforming to an approved-of stereoptype. After all the torrents of talk it was an oddly simple conclusion to arrive at.

The same principle probably applies to Arran. The most effective way to improve the quality of life for everyone is through individuals' decisions to do some small thing – and we're good at that. People take on unpaid jobs such as the providing of Helpline telephones, just because it's a way to make things a little bit better for someone. Or they take the trouble to write a letter about some obvious wrong, rather than leaving it to someone else. That, I suppose, is what Chomsky would call self determination, and it's the best way to achieve any improvement while we wait for the political theorists to catch up.

Exceptional swell

10 February 1990

WITH COFFEE MUGS sliding along the tables in the ferry cafeteria as the p.a. announced that we were heading for Gourock 'due to exceptional swell', I remember my first-ever incredibly rough crossing to Arran in 1939 with my intrepid grandmother – she had once frightened a tiger half to death by opening her parasol in his face when she met him on a jungle path, poor thing. (The tiger, I mean.)

How that paddle steamer bounced and tossed in the storm! In a downstairs saloon, stewardesses were handing out tin basins to the people who sat or lay on the plush maroon benches. It was very hot and crowded and everyone seemed to be vomiting. A woman with an ominously heaving Cairn terrier in her arms was demanding "a bowl for ma wee dog."

My grandmother surveyed the scene with some contempt. She was used, I suppose, to the superior arrangements of Cunard and P&O. "Fresh air," she ordered as I began to turn pale, and she propelled me up the cork-screwing stairs, preventing me from falling about by a powerful grip on my arm. There was some kind of remonstration from a crewman as she fought her way through the door into the lashing rain, holding me firmly in front of her. All signs of queasiness vanished at once in the wet wind. After a few minutes she said, "Right. Now we'll go and have dinner."

The chairs in the empty dining saloon were anchored by little chains to the floor and the tomato soup slid across the table from one brass edging rail to the other while I pursued it with spoon and bread roll. It was all very exhilarating.

Nowadays with stabilisers and propellers and a deeper draught to the boat, the crossing is never as rough. We have come to expect convenience, driving cars straight into the bowels of the ship instead of watching the spectacle as a crane manoeuvred a vehicle onto the deck as of yore. And yet, this blandness of modern travel has involved the sacrifice of much else. Powerless as they were to achieve a smooth crossing, the paddlers provided a far more comprehensive service than we enjoy today, as they pottered from Brodick to Lamlash and Whiting Bay and linking Blackwaterfoot with Campbeltown.

What's more, as a travelling environment, their meticulously constructed fittings of mahogany and brass and plush gave them an almost theatrical sense of occasion. Perhaps the very fact that sea-going passengers were likely to be exposed to quite a buffeting meant that the boats were built to seem cosy and reassuring and rather important.

Now the ferry is seen merely as a necessary interval between driving on the island and on the mainland. Despite the odd disaster in the English Channel, nobody seriously thinks the thing will not stay afloat. Theatricality and a sense of adventure have been banished in favour of the biggest possible vehicle deck and the cheapest possible plastic environment. This is an inevitable part of what is known as progress.

Perhaps it's all pure sentimentality. And yet, my happiest mornings are the non-ferry ones when I can walk the dogs up the glen and use up no energy except leg power. Funny thing, progress.

Grubbers and twitterers

24 February 1990

BIRD NUTS. THEY'RE A constant item on my shopping list in these winter months. For once the feathered friends find the free meals, they're in there like shoppers at sale time, grabbing all they can get. There's a fair amount of pushing and shoving (specially among the males of species, one can't help noticing!) and the whole system gets completely wrecked when the jackdaws arrive, armed with huge black beaks and feet like grappling irons. These brigands tear open the nets and gobble up the contents, watched by disconsolate bluetits.

But there's a shock waiting for them when they come back from foreign parts this spring, for the nuts are now dispensed in strong wire mesh holders. We'll see what that does for the heavy brigade.

Fortunately birds aren't human. If they were, the jackdaws would turn up equipped with bolt-croppers and bulldozers and a lot of money and continue to grab the lot, while the lesser beings scuffle about below them salvaging what they can. The human race has a depressing tendency to think that lack of power is a sign of inferiority. Jackdaws rule, OK?

You can see the jackdaw principle in operation on Arran rather clearly. We chirp at the tops of our bluetit voices about the need of a library, for instance – and what happens? Some bigger birds on the mainland get the money because they are louder and nearer to Great Peanut Provider. Arran's library was talked about for 1990. Now its being talked about for 1992. Talk is easy. Even parrots can do it. And so we are pretty-pollied from year to year with not so much as a sunflower seed.

Louder chirping obviously needed. It's been suggested that an extension of the service provided by the High School library could be taken up by the public – but this could easily be seen as a way out of having to provide a public library at all. Does anyone feel inclined to support a petition to the Council about it? If so, a few helpers will be needed to distribute petition forms. Drop a line to this column c/o the *Banner*.

Half the trouble with us bluetits of course, is that we twitter to our friends and neighbours about our complaints but seldom get together to do anything practical.

Take for instance the question of providing bins or bottle banks for the west side of the island. It seems absolutely unfair from their point of view that Brodick, Lamlash and Whiting Bay should hog the glass collection services so far provided. Agreed. Absolutely right. The problem is one of money. Every time a bottle bank is emptied, Thomson's lorry , at £20 an hour, has to go and lift it, dump the contents in the Brodick glass bay, then take it back. For journeys to the far side of the island the cost is going to be prohibitive.

Alternative plans are afoot. Thanks to Kiscadale Forge, we now have a home-made smaller version of a bottle bank. A prototype model can be seen outside Jim Lees' shop in Corrie. The contents of this could be transported by a small pick-up or even by a car and trailer. For £80 (which is a bargain compared with £500 for the Durabank), any village can have one. Run a jumble sale, buy a bottle bank?

But even on the car-and-trailer basis, the Arran Recycling Company can't do everything. To be honest, its workforce consists of three women, all of them with other occupations, who are desperately trying to cope with the whole thing.

To set up glass collection in Blackwaterfoot, Pirnmill, Shiskine etc, we must have some help from that side of the island. Is there anyone who can come from that area to Brodick with a van or trailer on a fairly regular basis? Or a few people who could take part in a rota? We need you!

Bluetits of the world unite!

Kicking up a stink

21 April 1990

THIS WEEK THERE have been complaints from the public (quite rightly) about the state of the Brodick foreshore where things consigned to lavatories are reappearing in large numbers. On top of this, many people have been pointing out with some indignation that the tanker which has been trundling round the island with the contents of people's septic tanks is disposing of said contents by pumping them out on an inadequately buried site on the unfortunate Brodick beach.

So what's the answer?

To a very large extent it is already there. We are manufacturing a lot of our own problems by failing to

understand the nature of the septic tank system. There's a tendency to think of a septic tank as a mere tank – a container which will gradually fill up with sewage until it needs pumped out. This is to miss the point.

A septic tank works because it is a digestive system. The bacteria which bring about the process we call 'rotting' are entirely familiar to gardeners who understand all about the way a huge pile of weeds and grass clippings gradually turns into a smaller one of compost. This too is a digestive process and it works because the bacteria in the pile are alive and well, working away like crazy. If however, a gardener was mad enough to soak the whole compost heap in bleach or disinfectant, the bacteria would be killed and the digestive process would stop.

It's exactly the same with the septic tank. Properly built and started off (an expert informs me that a dead rat works wonders!) , the digestive process can deal with all the sewage it is given. A septic tank should function for many years as a completely efficient system with clean water coming out at the far end of it. Many people have used septic tanks for years with no necessity at all for pumping out.

So what's this tanker doing?

Dealing with the users' mistakes, that's what it's doing. If a septic tank is abused with bleach and powerful lavatory cleaners and disinfectant, its bacteria will die, leaving an inert mass of stuff to accumulate until it is taken away somewhere else – where it still won't rot down properly.

It should of course be illegal for any household to discharge raw sewage and we can only wait for the local authorities to come to their senses about this. But while waiting, it must be

28

stressed that the septic tank system is no better unless it is properly used.

If you have a septic tank, you must not put bleach down the loo. Use a naturally-based cleaner such as Ecover instead. It works just as well, given a brisk brush. You can't expect the brown mark round the waterline to disappear of its own accord when the magic stuff is squirted in. And it's no use hankering after the operating theatre cleanliness which the Domestos ads suggest. Your loo can be perfectly clean but it does not have to be sterile. It's the passion for sterility which has led to all these dead septic tanks.

The other factor leading to tank death is washing powder. In the greasy old days before detergents were invented, very hot water was the biggest ally to the washer-up. Nowadays if the sink isn't crowned by a meringue of froth, the housewife feels obscurely unclean. But with washing machines and sinks all plumbed into the poor old septic tank, it doesn't get a chance.

The supermarkets are getting quite good at supplying washing products without phosphates. Look for the biodegradable labels and never mind the froth. If everyone can set their own septic tanks in order, a large part of the nasty problem with sewage will be taken care of. And then, aglow with virtue, we can kick up a stink – if that's the phrase – about households which, as primitively as a pig-sty, discharge raw sewage into the sea.

Adapt or perish

19 May 1990

I'M GLAD ARRAN news-
papers don't arrive at dawn,
hurled out of vans in great
bundles of depression. I can
with a clear conscience go for
a walk up the glen with the
dogs instead.

And what a pleasure it is
at the moment! The blue mist
of bluebells is beginning to
creep through the woods and
wild garlic is everywhere with
its wide open stars and its
heady smell. Every leaf and
blossom seems precisely
related to the conditions
which surround it. The
bluebells which grow at sea
level have been in bloom for
days but further up the hill,
where the temperature is a
little lower, the buds are still
tightly closed.

Half a mile or so up the burn, there is a big beech tree which lost a limb four or five years ago. It tore away from the main trunk and fell across the burn where the Forestry people tidied it up. The tree bears the scars of that massive injury but it is interesting to see how it has corrected its balance, growing new branches in such a way as to give itself maximum breathing space, yet putting no weight on the lower side of the bank where it grows.

This kind of intelligent adaptation happens everywhere. Dandelions regularly mowed in a lawn will manage to blossom as every gardener knows on stalks barely half an inch long, whereas they will reach a height of nearly a foot in an undisturbed shady situation. The mechanisms of this ability to adapt are unknown to us but the most seductively simple explanation lies in the idea that there is a 'rightness' in the world's natural relationships. Animals and plants – and perhaps we ourselves – are fundamentally aware of this right and have a vital instinct to fit in with it.

Darwin, modern biologists believe, got it wrong. His notion of the 'survival of the fittest' was a crude misinterpretation of a beautifully interlinked system. Being a Victorian and obsessed with the idea of gaining power over the environment, he assumed that all living creatures were playing the same game, thus setting up a suggestion of natural competitiveness which has lasted to the present day and which has done untold damage.

A more accurate phrase with which to sum up the way of the world is 'adapt or perish'. Seeds which fall in overcrowded places will not succeed because the pattern is already complete and so they cannot adapt to it. A bigger seed such as a sycamore may be able to do so simply because that environment may be able to accept a future tree whereas it cannot accept a daisy. It's not a matter of fighting, but of fitting in.

That's the great thing about dog-walks. They're full of fascinating revelations – which is more than can be said for newspapers.

Mad human disease

16 June 1990

JUST OCCASIONALLY, writers of columns such as this one get stopped in the street for pats on the back on something which has tickled the public fancy. In recent weeks, top of the Green pops has been the piece on septic tanks which seem to be amazingly close to the Arran heart. Everyone had righteous views on the folly of putting bleach into what should be a bacterially-functioning system.

I suppose it's a question of 'striking home' as they say. There's nothing much nearer to home than sewage. It's much more difficult to feel truly involved in some mythical hole somewhere in the sky. This week though, I feel bothered about the sea which

is a pretty familiar neighbour to all of us on Arran – or indeed if you look at it in wider terms – to the mainland and to most countries of the world, since the sea is common to all of us everywhere.

Scotland on Sunday carried a story this week which filled me with gloom. It is reported that the Ministry for Fisheries and Food is about to issue a further two year licence for the use of Aquagard in fish farms. What is Aquagard? It is Nuvan tricked out in a new name, rather like Winscale changed into Sellafield after a fire which nearly blew the place sky-high. Ciba-Geigy will do very nicely out of the new licence and the fish farmers will be able to go on battling against the diseases which affect their caged and unnatural stock.

You'd think we'd learn. Every single one of these intensive monocultures – perpetual wheat, battery hens, protein-stuffed cattle, farmed fish – every single one comes up with its own array of diseases and failures. After some years of smallholding in Suffolk, I saw exactly what happened to the fields of my larger-scale farming neighbours who moaned continually about expensive fertiliser leaching away in the rain (through soil which was no more than sand and dust) and lost crops every year through 'lodging' when wind and rain flattened the barley precariously rooted in the insubstantial earth. And last year we all saw eggs being bulldozed into pits. Why? Basically because chickens were fed on pellets partially composed of the diseased corpses of their fellows.

Mad Human Disease seems to be rampant. Only mad humans could seriously contemplate feeding bullocks on the brains of sheep. It is such a disgusting idea that the industry fully deserves the come-uppance which nature is handing out.

And what about these fish farms? At the moment they look harmless enough – just a few rafts floating in the sea causing no great visual offence. The question of what is going on underneath them is something else. In Grantown-on-Spey a farm has recently been closed because of bacterial kidney disease. Nine tons of salmon were destroyed. Ten tons have been destroyed in Wester Ross, Lewis and Shetland. Just imagine how many individual fish there are in a ton.

The Marine Conservation Society is worried. Alison Ross, their Scottish conservation officer says, "The antibiotics and chemical treatment that are used have potentially damaging but as yet largely unknown effects on the wider environment and there is now clear evidence that some pathogens have become resistant to treatment."

You cannot go on tipping dichlorvos into the sea without mucking up the balance of its bacterial life any more than you can bung bleach into the septic tank and expect it to go on working. In the case of the misused septic tank you can get a firm to pump it out and pump the sludge in pits in Brodick (poor old Brodick, does it really deserve this?) but in the case of the sea, there is no tanker big enough to remove the results of the damage. As islanders the least we can do is to boycott farmed salmon. Who wants dichlorvos, anyway?

Inconvenience

15 July 1990

"MAY I BE EXCUSED?" we used to say at school when a need of nature made itself felt. And oh the agony if the teacher frowned and said, "You should have gone before. Wait until playtime."

The feeling came flooding back – oh dear no, wrong choice of words – the feeling was sharply recalled last week when I noticed a little queue of visitors outside the super-loo in Whiting Bay, shifting unobtrusively from foot to foot as they stared out to sea valiantly. One man was whistling a little tune through his teeth.

Everybody at some time or other has known the discomfort of a full bladder. It is one of the most universal human experiences. The City of Cardiff is marked for ever in my mind as a ghastly place because, emerging one night in the company of a Rugby team from a pub which had no Ladies (and precious few ladies either), I walked for miles and agonising miles in search of a welcoming open door scented with wonderful Jeyes Fluid and finally had to take refuge in a Gents while the prop forward stood guard outside the door.

All civilised places should offer the convenience of Conveniences. They should be central, ever-open and, unless they are to employ an attendant supplied with handfuls of change, they should also be free. On this basis, Arran is not civilised. The narrow brown boxes are a kind of toilet-substitute, a baffling joke-toilet devised, one feels, by a researcher in behaviourism who lurks round corners with binoculars and a Mr Whippy watching the effects of his brainchild on the public. "Aha! Zey are lookink at ze little green light!" (All mad scientists have to be some sort of obscure Central European.) "Now zey read ze words. Too bad zey are forgettink ze glasses, ha-ha."

Elderly ladies have been seen poking hopefully at the control buttons. Others shake their heads as if being asked to go on the Big Dipper – and who knows that they might not be right? Folk legend has left the Three Old Ladies who had trouble with their suspenders far behind and now concentrates on dark tales of The Man Who Stayed In Too Long. The children insert a coin into the slot and then stake a step back in fascinated alarm rather as if they have pressed the Go button on a Dalek.

There is, I suppose, some entertainment value about the things but seriously, this is no way to cater for the need of several thousand people. All else apart, the provision is nowhere near enough. When the brown boxes cease to function (which they have already done several times) the provision is nil.

Council representatives seem immensely proud of their joke-toilets because they are vandal-proof. It's a bit sad about the Council, really, the way they regard the public as a bunch of barbarians who cost money just by existing – but one can see their point in a way. It's very depressing to get things smashed up. Some idiot even hurled a picnic table over the Glen Ashdale Falls a few weeks ago and the Forestry Commission are understandably reluctant to supply another one. But toilets with tiled walls and doors which are sprung to stay open unless bolted shut from inside do not offer much of a refuge to the graffiti-artist or the destruction maniac.

The Council really should think again on this one. And if Arran residents or visitors agree that we deserve a better service than the strong brown Autoloo, please write to the Council and tell them so. Drop a sea-side postcard to Cunninghame House, Irvine. At least it will interest the mad scientist.

Seeing things afresh

28 July 1990

IN THE SUMMER, IT IS very nice to pretend you are on holiday even if you are not. This could be difficult in Walsall or Wandsworth but on Arran there is nothing to overcome except one's own inertia. On a sunny Saturday afternoon one can play at being a tourist.

Lots of people do it. Worthy citizens sit in cafes in a positively Mediterranean state of undress and I know a teenager who bought a bucket and spade as soon as the school term ended. The great thing is, it brings about a completely fresh appreciation of the island – specially if somebody else does the driving. Installed in the car with the dogs as excited as toddlers in the back and towels for sandy feet and a rug for sitting on, off we go. "Goodness, isn't it different round this side. . ." Any minute now, we're going to get the lecture about the benevolent influence of the Gulf Stream.

Really, though, there does seem to be a mental trick about looking at things anew. Why had I not noticed before how quiet Lochranza is? The hills seem to swallow up all sound and when a car has been past, the silence comes after it and hushes the engine noise with its peace. And what pleasure can be greater than sitting on a rug and staring as if for the first time at a sparkling, milky-calm sea and the line of hills with a blue sky and a few white wisps of cloud?

And then there's paddling. You can't be a proper, old-fashioned seaside postcard tourist without paddling, skirts held up and whoops-a-daisy as a sudden wave sends the cold water to unexpected heights. It's a different thing from all that splashing and gasping and clutching the arms about the shoulders which goes with swimming. Paddling is a delicate, exploratory occupation, not so much a soaking of the feet as a scientific investigation, involving the holding up of dripping specimens of wild life and peering at them closely.

This particular Saturday it was hermit crabs – tiny ones, inhabiting the smallest possible winkle shells. On the palm, they poke out a bunch of almost translucent small legs and claws then, appalled by the sunlight, pulled them in again. Once replaced in the water (upside down, just for the fun of watching what happens) the legs come out, dig into the sand and in a flash the little crab is shell-side up again. Dozens of them were making their solemn way over the ridged sand under six inches of water, going out with the tide so that they should not be left high and dry.

With a continuance of the quasi-scientific spirit, I reflected wistfully on the wonderfully renewable housing system of hermit crabs, who simply move out of a shell when it gets too small and find a new one. It must be a worrying time when the current shell is getting to be a tight squeeze and a bigger one has not happened along. Humans at least don't run the risk of being eaten if they are in a state of temporary homelessness but they do have all the bother about getting a mortgage or affording the rent or finding a house at all.

As organisms which consider ourselves vastly more sophisticated than hermit crabs, you'd think humans would have cracked all those problems years ago. Surely we could have come up with a benevolent system of small winkle shells for beginner-crabs? There used to be Council houses of course, but those all got sold off. . .

Interestingly, in Whiting Bay, all the winkle shells are owner-occupied. Not a hermit crab in sight. No analogies intended or even imagined. Over here, it's more difficult to see things afresh. But I'm working on it.

41

Thinking with your feet

11 August 1990

WHEN ONE'S CAR HAS A heart attack, the effects are far-reaching. The stricken car itself of course, is perfectly happy. It relaxes into a prolonged rest cure while a gear-box donor is sought – and the owner walks. And walks.

It's been very enjoyable, rediscovering feet. They've always been useful for plodding up the glen with the dogs in the mornings but in the last couple of months my pedal extremities, as Fats Waller called them, have come into their own. Going for the papers has become an art form. Not only is it necessary to remember whether it's an early-boat day or a late-boat day but the state of the tide is to be considered.

There is no point in walking along a road in the backwash of other people's exhaust fumes (oh how noisy and smelly cars are when one is outside them!) if the beach is available instead. And there is no point in walking along a beach in shoes. Sooner or later, a puddle is stepped in and white watermarks later appear on the leather, or newish trainers very quickly turn into old ones.

No, the only way to walk along a beach is in bare feet. At first the poor things flinch and cringe like raw recruits on their first assault course but they soon cheer up. In just a few days, they are taking barnacle-covered rocks in their stride as you might say. And the sense of well-being is terrific.

There is, after all, a whole science of bodily improvement based on massage of the feet. Each little bit is reckoned to have its equivalent in some other part of you just as acupuncture works through the mysterious network of canals called meridians which convey energy around. I sometimes have visions of the scummier stretches of the Grand Union and feel that my meridians are similarly stagnant and full of the results of nasty habits – but beach walking has changed all that.

The other nice thing about being a pedestrian is that you feel part of the place you are walking through. In a car, it is just the view outside. It's curious though, how this sense of participation varies from season to season. Walking up Glen Ashdale (with shoes on or wellies) there is a tremendous feeling of identification with the place from about October onwards, increasing in March and April to a positively exuberant connection. It's difficult to know what this feeling really is, but many people will know it from long experience. There is a sense of sharing in the way a natural place knows how to run its own affairs, and it produces a kind of reassurance that the world will continue to manage itself when humankind has gone all the way along its crazy path to oblivion.

Oddly, several people have agreed lately that a change happens towards the end of June. After the bluebells have gone and the great brassy kingcups have disappeared from the soggy places by the burn there seems to be an in-turning, a retreat into privacy. The place feels neutral and preoccupied. I am inclined to think that this is because everything is pregnant. The beech tree broods quietly over its thousands of triangular seeds and the brambles are forming berries within their tatty white flowers. The hawthorn that was full of creamy blossom in May is making its bunches of little pale green fruits. This is their work and they do it as well as they can. It takes all their energy.

Later, when berries have ripened and the beech mast has turned brown, there seems to be a sense of relief. Everything settles into winter almost as the island's humans do, with enjoyment of communication now that the main work of the year is completed. But maybe it is all fanciful and the result of too much stimulation of the meridians. Perhaps my feet have gone to my head.

Poisonous

25 August 1990

DURING MY FARMING years, the dog was very keen on what the children called 'mice lollies'. With a rather stiff tail sticking out of the front of her mouth, she would wander about sucking contentedly at a small corpse. She ate birds at a gulp but never ate mice or rats. Perhaps that's one of the reasons why she is still alive, unlike many less for-tunate animals.

Mice can be killers. No, they do not go for the jugular or perform Tom and Jerry tricks with trip wires and exploding sardines – they kill much more innocently than that. With no malevolence whatever, they pass on the death which a human being has induced in them. A poisoned mouse does not curl

up and die as soon as it has taken the bait. Warfarin acts quite slowly, destroying the clotting function of the blood. The mouse becomes a haemophiliac and dies eventually from internal bleeding. While this is happening, it will continue to lead its life in the normal way though slowed down by feeling very ill.

Sick mice are easier to catch than healthy mice, so cats find the sufferers an easy prey. They gobble up a nice little supper of mouse (and the Warfarin which is in its stomach) and come in to wash their faces by the fire. But there are a lot of sick mice out there, and in a week or two an efficient hunting cat will have ingested a lot of second-hand Warfarin. Then the cat too becomes a haemophiliac. It seems tired, is disinclined to eat, loses weight and moves more slowly. Its body temperature drops and if inspected, the inside of its eyelids will be white, indicating acute anaemia. Once it feels cold to the touch of your hand, it usually dies within forty-eight hours.

A lot of beloved pets are dying this way. Young, healthy cats are the best hunters, so they are the most vulnerable to this second-hand poisoning. It's a sad thing to happen to a family, specially where there are children. And these deaths are needless.

How else can mice and rats be controlled? In the house, a good cat is perfectly capable of doing the job. A neutered female usually makes the best hunter. Householders who don't want to own a cat can deal with the odd mouse by setting the old-fashioned mousetrap. It kills instantly and humanely, without the long drawn out suffering caused by poisoning and what's more, you won't have little corpses decomposing in hidden-away places, causing flies and nasty smells.

If you are not a murderer by inclination but still don't want mouse footprints in the butter dish, a single invader is quite easily caught and returned to the great outdoors by the welly boot method. A panic stricken mouse will flee for shelter into a dark hole, so lay your welly-boot on its side in a corner and chase the mouse towards it. The mouse will dive in and go right down to the toe. Pick the boot up and shake the occupant out in the garden. If wellies are left on their sides overnight, check them for contents before putting them on in the morning or your toes may encounter a surprise.

Rats are a larger problem, specially in the autumn when they tend to come into farm buildings after harvest. Being such prolific breeders, they create population explosions. Again, a staff of farm cats must be the first answer, but in old buildings with a lot of refuge places, an occasional purge may be necessary. We used to have a shoot with a couple of dogs to help. Cage-type traps, well-baited, also work very well because rats are always hungry when there are too many of them.

All technicalities apart, a sense of proportion is needed. Rats and mice, left to themselves, are clean and fastidious animals always washing and grooming themselves. They do not carry the Black Death in this day and age, neither do they run up your skirt (though it is wise to tuck your trousers into your boots before mounting an offensive). They have been in the world as long as we have and a reasonable balance between us can be achieved. There is no need at the sight of a mouse to engage in chemical warfare which can bring suffering and death to other people's pets. Please think before you poison.

Autumn

22 September 1990

AFTER THE SLEEPINESS of August, autumn seems to bring a new burst of activity. With the shortening daylight and the crispness in the mornings, there's rolling up of sleeves going on in preparation for the coming winter. Humans must be aware of it as well – why else should the academic year begin when the summer is over?

On Arran, as the visitors drift homeward, there is a particular briskness. Leaves patter down in the woods and the brambles ripen and there is a sense of duty done. Everyone – and perhaps everything – feels slightly different.

A few days ago the swallows gathered on the telephone wire outside my window, twittering and fluttering and setting their feathers in order, rushing up into little flights and then returning to perch again, giving themselves little shakes like high jumpers poised at the run-up. And across on a neighbouring roof, the house martins were holding a meeting of their own, dotted about on the sun-warmed slates and babbling to each other like budgies.

And then they were gone. The next morning, there was a touch of frost and the roof where they had gathered was shadowed and cold. A few remain, twittering uncertainly – young ones, so the naturalists say, left to follow a few days later. We theorise about magnetic sensors and direction-finding capacity, but the fact that these small birds go away on this long journey and come back again to exactly the same spot remains magical. However it is done, there is an element of world citizenship about it.

The beach too, seems full of activity. Jellyfish are arriving in their hapless sort of way, to get stranded on the sand rather like somebody who needs a hand to get up out of a sagging deck chair. They bumble about in the shallow water of the receding tide, making vague efforts to pump themselves seaward but each ripple throws them back to the shore. And there they sit, plump and purple and embarrassed, waiting to be rescued by the next tide. In the winter, I have seen them frozen as solid as Pyrex plates – but that still lies ahead.

Crabs are of much more sparky personality than jellyfish and don't get washed ashore unless they are dead. But why are there so many small dead crabs? Among the rocks and along the water's edge there is always a scatter of them. It is a small worry to add to all the others. And yet, there is a feeling that crabs will probably be around when humans have muddled themselves into extinction, and it is obscurely comforting.

Little fish abound in the shallow water left on the beach. Only about half an inch long, they dart about in the water, regardless of the fact that the pools are fed by the little burns of fresh water which come down from the hill. This puzzles me. Does anyone know what these fishlets are? No matter what their identity, it's good to see them there – and last week to spot a four inch long flattie scuttling through shallow water just above the sand.

Remembering pre-war summers on Arran, the fishing fleets come back to mind, a dozen or more boats with tyres along their sides as fenders, each with a red-brown stay-sail. There were fish then, in a big way. Where have all the fishes gone? People caught them, every one. . . And in Lowestoft I have seen women refused a single fish for their families' teas because the catch had failed to make a high price at auction and the whole gleaming pile of it was going from the quayside to be turned into fertiliser.

The oldest fishermen of all do not waste anything. The herons stand on big stones in the water as slim as Greek vases, waiting patiently, and last week, a basking shark was wandering about by the rocks outside Whiting Bay Primary School mopping up a bit of plankton and – well – basking. Long may it continue.

The wee Arran all-star

17 November 1990

ON ARMISTICE Sunday, it is strange to have flamboyant Oriental poppies coming into fat bud in the garden. The remembrance of war and its futility seems set in November's greyness and mud, not in this determined bursting forth of life. Nasturtiums flourish their trumpets and marigolds bloom doggedly on – there was even a single mad blossom on the montana clematis last week.

On Arran, in common with most country places, the weather and its effects can't be ignored. We venture out and look at the sky with appreciation or disgust, walk only a few paces from the house and notice how the short sharp frost of last week has licked the bracken into shape, cutting down its green cockiness to a brown and grovelling obedience. That's our reality. And yet, in the space of a few hours, a completely different reality can be just as immediate. All you have to do is get on the ferry and keep going.

Take for instance our own, our very own Johnny McGovern, star turn of a gathering which arrived to welcome him home from New York. For a week, he'd been in a setting as far removed from autumnal Whiting Bay as you could imagine and there he was, in a Marathon Finishers tee-shirt to prove it, rambling on about hamburger joints and some place called the Emerald Isle Bar.

With the avid curiosity of out-of-town hicks, we questioned him about the Big Apple. Was it as violent as everyone said? (I'd only just found out that Central Park was bigger than the grassed-over George Square which I'd always imagined.) Had he seen anyone shot, mugged, robbed, arrested? Were the cops as tough as everyone said?

"Great guys," Johnny said, with just a touch of the Bronx in his ripe Paisley accent. When he got lost in some avenue that looked like all other avenues, he asked two of them the way back to the Youth Hostel. "Louie and Gomez. Great guys. They took me back there in the cop car."

"Screaming sirens?" we asked, agog.

"Oh aye, screaming sirens. They turned up in civvies later on, took me out for a drink."

And there had been a sequel. When Our Hero had begun to flag a little in the last stages of the race itself, in the humid heat of a New York Indian summer, he trotted past Gomez, uniformed and on duty. "He pulled this huge gun out and said, "Shift your ass, Scottie, or I'll blow your goddam head off." It must be a wonderful training method – Arran's human greyhound clocked a personal best and came in very respectably in the first few thousand finishers. They do things in a big way in New York.

It sounds a funny place, though. Halloween produced a massive parade and business men were sitting in the subway wearing city suits and wild make-up. Do such celebrations get more approved-of or less as they get bigger, I wonder? Perhaps the ancient tradition of celebrating winter's onset with apples and nuts and a small taunting of the spirits of evil assumes a big commercial recognition once it becomes a profitable business., But you can't keep good magic down. When the wee Arran All-Star came travelling home on the train from London, the tee-shirt again worked wonders and he fetched up sitting in First Class luxury with a middle-aged American fairy godmother pouring out the champagne. But then of course, the guard was from Glasgow. . .

So here we are, in the November Arran days, but with a tiny insight into the reality of New York, where the Statue of Liberty is floodlit red white and blue because of the threatened conflict in the Gulf. Some realities remain unthinkable. As Johnny says, "I hope they don't nuke the Emerald Isle Bar." Not to mention Louie and Gomez.

Seasonable

15 December 1990

"SEASONABLE," someone said briskly the other day when we met, as red-nosed as a couple of Rudolphs in the Post Office. Jingle bells and ho, ho, ho. In the bleak mid-winter, we are all supposed to be dreaming of a White Christmas, and the weather is currently doing its best to be festive.

Green principles take a bashing at Christmas. After eleven and a half months of re-using envelopes and buying recycled toilet paper instead of the decadent coloured stuff, decent self-limitation melts away like a snowflake on a carol singer's lantern. It's the same every year – the determination to keep calm and make a reasonable list of presents and stick

to it – and what happens? Conscience creeps in. Will Aunt Maud really be happy with a slim volume called 50 Ways to Save the Planet? Maybe she'd better have an ethnic silk scarf as well. But in that case, a bottle of Evening of Primrose hair restorer won't be enough for Uncle Willoughby. Perhaps he could have a Rainforest tee-shirt instead. But then what would I do with. . .

There's no end to it. A remorseless levelling-up has set in and what started as a token gift-giving turns into a real effort to do the thing right. It's the same with food. Reason flies out of the frost-sprayed windows as a kind of panic sets in. Will there be enough? People may fancy fresh fruit rather than all that heavy stuff, and maybe a salad – but then Andy likes his potatoes and gravy. One must provide what is wanted. Providing becomes a fetish. At this darkest time of the year, there is a feeling of wanting the house to contain a good store, so that it can survive for a while even if the snow does lie about deep and crisp and even.

Underlying the shopping expeditions and the laying-in of stores there is an ancient sense of the winter as a time of siege. The sun comes reluctantly above the slope of the hill to cast a sleepy red-eyed gaze at the scene and then go away again to more favoured parts of the world. In spite of knowing that its warmth will in the fullness of time increase again, there's a trace of desperation about the dark days. It must have seemed doubly so in times long past.

Christmas itself is of ancient pre-Christmas origin. The Julian calendar reckoned that the winter solstice fell on December 25 and felt that the days began to lengthen from that date onward. The priests of the Mithraic religion celebrated the birth of the sun god's new year on December 25 by coming from an inner shrine with a loud cry of "The light is waxing!" and the image of an infant child was brought out to show the worshipper that the sun was newly born. In Syria and Egypt, this celebration went on for a long time after the birth of Christ, which Egyptian Christians came to regard as being on January 6 in the absence of any guidance on the matter from the Gospels.

After some three hundred years of Mithraic jollifications on December 25, the Christians sensibly decided to opt for the same date, though the change was not adopted at Antioch until the year 375AD.

So much for the useless facts department. Meanwhile, walking up the glen on these cold mornings remains a delight. The icy puddles crack into star shapes when trodden on and each grass blade is coated with fuzzy whiteness. There is a strange contentedness about the place, turned in on itself like a cat's paws as it drowses before a winter fire. It is resting with the stores of beech mast and pine cones completed for the dual purposes of continuing tree life through seeding and animal life through feeding. As the winter sun comes up behind the trees, there is a quiet certainty that, quite soon now, the days will start to lengthen and growth will begin again. No matter to whom or to what this continuing miracle is ascribed, it is surely something to celebrate. Merry Christmas.

Storms and sewage

12 January 1991

CONSIDERING THAT we are islanders, it is surprisingly easy most of the time to ignore the presence of the sea. It is there as a background, the straight grey line seen between trees or glimpsed in the dip of a hill, just as there is a Tuscan landscape behind the Mona Lisa. But the smile on the face is more commanding that the cypress trees and distant mountain range and so the background remains background.

Just occasionally it moves into much more dramatic focus, hogging the limelight like a neglected understudy. There were signs of it as the old year changed to the new, watched by a full moon so huge that it managed to dwarf a night of kissing and dancing and carousing into insignificance. At half past seven in the morning it was still there, sailing on like (I suppose) a mega-star, lofty and assured and much more impressive than any quantity of booze.

Since then the sea has been decidedly skittish. Boats have barely been permitted to set keel in it and on the twelfth day of Christmas it staged a pantomime which had us all spell-bound. There was no hope of doing anything else but watch it, hoping not to be singled out for special attention like a hapless member of the audience in the stalls who gets his braces stolen by the conjuror.

It was a tremendous show. The spray came crashing in like fireworks and water thundered through the Glenashdale bridge with barely space to spare, thumping into the wall with a noise like collapsing blocks of flats. It has changed the landscape at Whiting Bay, tearing away the green and chunks of the wall, piling stones by the ton all over the road and burying the putting green in piles of shingle and rock.

Our high-tech skills were quite useless while all this was going on. There was nothing to be done except deploy the odd sandbag and pray that the electricity didn't pack up. There was something quite primitive about such helplessness. People must have felt the same when they sheltered in broch and fort and cleat, keeping out of the way of the murderous hail of water and rocks. Being more careful than we are (because the careless did not survive) they will have wondered if they had done something wrong to merit such a furious punishment. In the morning, treading fearfully among the strewn weed and spray-flung stone, there would be promises to try harder and to atone for any unwitting offence which had been committed.

Logic assures us that such connections between cause and effect are groundless. There was no blame and there is no need for repentance and expiation. Or is there?

True, we do not cause a storm. And a freak high tide cannot be connected to any specific ecological sin. But when the sea moves suddenly into the foreground, it seems natural enough to give it some attention. Even if the offences we cause do not result in direct retribution, they are nonetheless offences – and sooner or later they must be recognised or they will lead to disaster.

Take for instance, the question of sewage. The Council, for some reason best known to itself, is following a policy of putting all new buildings on what they grandly call 'the mains'. This means that sewage goes into the officially provided pipe that discharges it untreated into the sea. The next high tide very sensibly returns it to us by depositing it back on the beaches. Longer pipes discharge it further out, to try and force the sea to accept and digest it. How much do we imagine it can deal with? Do we go on increasing the load until a point of total breakdown is reached?

On this island, domestic sewage is free of the heavy metals that contaminate it in areas where industrial plant discharges into the system, so it is ideal for treatment and use as fertiliser. Septic tanks, properly used without bleach and detergent, are an efficient way of treating sewage to provide a harmless run-off of clean water. Anyone concerned about our continued sea-dumping should urge the Council to reconsider its policy. We never outgrow the need to be careful.

Toilet training

26 January 1991

BEING AN AVID reader can have its disadvantages. My mother, unwrapping fish and chips, would on occasion be struck with infuriating slowness as she perused a previously overlooked article in the greasy and crumpled *News Chronicle*. It's an atavistic tendency – as my mother's daughter, I in turn was struck motionless when supposed to be shaking the doormat outside the kitchen, arrested by something in the newspaper that underlay the mat to catch the dust.

It's just as bad now. Putting a newly bought four-pack of recycled toilet paper in the bathroom shelf the other day, I was caught by the consumer information

printed on the wrapper. All good stuff, I thought, smugly perusing the details. Made from 100% recycled office paper, unbleached, conserving woodland, average 240 sheets per roll, total area 14 square metres. WHAT? It's about the size of a suburban garden.

All complacency shrivelled away. Several times a year, I personally am putting 14 square metres of loo paper into the sea, via what the Council laughingly calls the sewage system. Its enough to induce chronic constipation.

My mind flitted back to a trip to Morocco about six years ago, when the family all seemed to be doing something else at Christmas and I went off for a bit of exploring in the Atlas mountains. A village bed-and-breakfast in Morocco (where you get given a padlock for your door) does not have a flush toilet, much less any form of loo paper. Instead, as in all third world countries a large pan of water stands outside the door, together with a dipper – usually a gallon plastic container with the top sawn off. (Empty plastic containers are sold in the markets.) You take your dipper of water into the cubicle with you and use it, with fingers as necessary, pouring the last of the water over your hand and then coming out for another scoopful to flush down the French-type hole.

Since the use of water is all one-way, it's a very clean system. Hands are washed under running water and one habitually eats with one hand and cleans with the other. There is intense curiosity about the nasty habits of Europeans who are reputed to use dry paper alone.

We have a very strong taboo about the bodily functions. So much so that it is probably quite impossible to suggest to any 'civilised' European whose toilet contains a wash basin that a little sponge and warm water might do the job rather pleasantly and save the odd fourteen square metres of paper. Dash it, there are limits!

Turning to more orthodox reading matter, I have just finished Umberto Eco's *The Name of the Rose* which is in one way a whodunnit. It is set in a Benedictine monastery in the thirteenth century and intricately interwoven with theological argument. For anyone of Green inclinations, the theme it develops is a fascinating one. The monastery is obsessed with purity of thought and subservience to the will of God – there is an almost hysterical pursuit of goodness. This demands an eschewing of the imperfect reality that exists in the outside world and it also requires a strict limiting of the mind. A dedicated monk, the argument goes, must not entertain the thoughts of the less-than-perfect humans who live untidy lives and write books containing irreverent ideas. The monastery's magnificent library is forbidden territory, for the freedom expressed in its volumes is seen as the work of the Antichrist.

Without giving away the plot, I can reveal that fanaticism proves itself in the end to be untenable. The peas-in-the-sandals approach to a good cause gives you nothing but sore feet. For a book devoted to sanctity, it's a helluva good read.

Wild longings

23 February 1991

THINGS ARE ON THE move again. In the hard frost there was a sense of suspended animation, as if nothing could move until the softer air came and released us from the spell. It's odd, come to think of it, how freezing really means stillness. 'Freeze-frame' – and the moving figures in a film are static images. A person frozen with horror is struck motionless, just as the frozen water in the burn is brought to a standstill and turns white and stiff.

Last week the stones where the dipper bobs in the summer like a swimmer on the brink were transformed into strange white things like iced buns with paper doyleys round them, and the running water was hidden under a

frozen carpet of fern-patterned ice. It was weirdly beautiful, but the robins and wrens flitted from branch to branch in hungry anxiety, coming quite close to watch the dogs in hopes that the dafter one of the two would dig up a stone to play with and expose some fresh, scratchable earth. 'Grubby' suddenly had a new meaning as I thought about it from the robins' point of view, and I took to carrying a bagful of currants and crumbs and bits of cold potato in my pocket. Then the rain came and the birds' security returned.

Rain comes down, water vapour goes up. On a sunny day the puddles steam. The wind rushes about, the burn runs, the sea comes in and goes out, everything moves. Bluebells' shoots are coming up, the red petals of premature primulas are going down into the tummies of sparrows, snowdrops are out. The whole thing is galloping along, impelled by the turning of the world, and the days lengthen quickly, stretching out towards the spring.

Everything around us is on the move except the humans. For some reason we don't accept that this constant state of natural movement and change includes ourselves. We get so obsessed with the idea of stability and security that we spend a lot of time making rules and then spend a whole lot more time obeying them. And yet our chief delight is in the pure pleasure of living, with no restrictions or duties to spoil it. A good holiday is one where you can do exactly as you please, preferably in a beautiful 'unspoilt' place. At heart, we want to be the children of nature – and yet we disapprove of that very desire. Proper grown-ups don't have such wild longings, we tell ourselves.

Children, on the other hand, belong absolutely in the way things are. There is a wonderful drawing on the wall of

Bannatyne's Office in Blackwaterfoot, done by someone quite small. It is called 'Granny's Rat' and it is green and rat-shaped and whiskery and I very much admire Granny for having such a splendid animal and the young artist for drawing it. No rules or dutiful pieces of obedience could have produced anything so lively - it's an expression of the ratness of rat and the childness of child in a little bit of the worldness of the world. And I bet Granny had a hand in it too.

This delightful rat-viewing experience happened when I went with a member of the Arran Recycling Company to buy a van, more efficiently to collect empty bottles from pubs. At present, one of the smallest cars on the island totters to and from the coup with load after small load of glass, doing more miles than necessary and burning more fuel and taking up more driver-time. The new van is an obvious improvement. In other ways, though, the Recycling Company is looking at a rather bleak future. Although Blue Boxes have arrived like manna from heaven, there is a desperate shortage of people to deploy them. Due to the various plans and ambitions of the little band of Recyclers, it looks as if their total number may be down to two by the coming summer. A rather desperate letter from Samantha Boorer in last week's *Banner* produced just one offer of help (for which, many thanks).

To stay on the move, this enterprise needs a few more active people only about once a month. Otherwise, a strange stillness is going to overtake the Bottle Bus, a freezing into immobility even in the balmy days of summer.

The great high tide

9 February 1991

WALKING ALONG THE sea wall in Whiting Bay, it is impossible not to notice the cracks that have appeared in it since the Great High Tide. Some of them are old ones, moss-grown and unmoving, but far more are new, showing clean edges of broken stone where whole sections have shifted a little. The next storm will finish what the last one began.

The power of the water is frightening. Looking at the sea out there twinkling gently in the sun, it is like a bad dream to remember it hurling rocks and weed across the road. I fish out the photographs and look and remember the violence of that strange afternoon. It was a demonstration of natural

power, as if laid on by some cosmic salesman. "And here we have the Super De Luxe Model for those who require a little extra. . ."

It's quite odd to think that there is all that power moving around out there and yet we get our knickers in such a twist trying to supply ourselves with power in our houses and factories and cars. Our approach to this is weirdly primitive. Like children who understand pennies in the hand but have no conception of a bank balance, we turn to tangible stuff which can be dug and burned just as our ancestors reached for dead branches or turf or peat. We still seem to want stuff we can see and weigh and get our hands dirty with. Coal, being splendidly black and heavy, fits the bill perfectly and oil, though it runs about in a rather modern way, is equally tangible and satisfactory and besides it can be made into plastic objects of all sorts. Uranium, despite its touch of space-fiction magic, still has a certain kind of solidness and the fact that it has to be kept cool with thousands of gallons of water gives it undeniable presence.

Water itself, on the other hand, has always seemed too common to bother with. Only in comparatively recent times have we harnessed the power of waterfalls to give us hydroelectricity, and the sea remains its own self, a wild thing which is useful only as a devourer of sewage. Some years ago, a group of scientists invented a natty device known as a duck which rather naturally floated in the water and produced power from its goings up and down. Strangely, the efficiency of the duck was seriously misrepresented by official channels and despite the anguish of its proud parents it was never taken seriously.

The same thing has happened over wind-power statistics.

67

There has been an odd reluctance to admit that this free energy which blows about the sky could be economically harnessed and used. All sorts of conspiracy theories are tempting – vested interests must not be upset, the commitment to nuclear weapons must be honoured (if one can use so decent a word in such an obscene service). But it may be that we overlook the most significant factor of all – namely, the collective 'feeling' about fuel which we have inherited unthinkingly from our ancient ancestors.

Being Great British Islanders, we perhaps have an insular dependence on the very stuff of our right little tight little island. We do not let go of the imagination and blow with the wind or surge with the sea. We grasp at what we regard as 'facts' and make inflexible rules. Coal and oil fit in well with this passion for the substantive. They can be handled and weighed and they are there, solid and inert, beneath the earth, waiting to be dug out or tapped. We do not like the idea that we could put ourselves at the mercy of the winds that blow. It is not scientific objection but a psychological one.

If mass prejudice is in fact the product of collective thought rather than of any scientific rationale, then what we all think really matters.

Dr John Twidell, who directs the Energy Studies Unit at Strathclyde University, said in a letter to the *Glasgow Herald* last week, "Scotland has the best wind energy potential in the whole of Europe. . . Such energy is produced with no chemical pollution and no carbon dioxide. With all costs included, wind power is probably the cheapest form of new electricity." But the energy of thought costs nothing at all. Keep at it!

Grass – as short as a sergeant's hair

20 April 1991

WHEN THE SUN SHINES with real warmth in these wonderful midge-free spring days, it takes almost masochistic self-discipline to stay at the typewriter. It is so much nicer to wander greenly outside and poke about in the garden. Looking at the bucketful of wilting dandelions and couch grass and long stalked dry-looking things with minuscule white flowers on top, I had a pang of conscience. Gardening is such a fascist occupation really, selecting the chosen and rejecting the unfortunate others. And yet, God wot, a garden is a lovesome thing and there is something amazingly soothing to the

soul about a harmonious community of plant life.

It's very odd that we are so confident about what is ugly in a garden. Nobody confesses a secret liking for a bold sweep of ground elder, or feels that intermittent nettle clumps among the pinks are a pleasing feature. Even wild gardeners (that is to say, the cultivators of wild gardens - I don't mean to imply that they dance a mad fandango among their Mr Fothergill kingcups) even draw the line at bramble and sow-thistle. All gardening is a process of selecting the most pleasing possibility from an almost infinite range. It is probably the last of the arts to survive as a genuine, unselfconscious means of expression.

The artistic arts have, in my view, been infected by a kind of aesthetic AIDS which has undermined their health. There is an obsession with the status of the artist as performer which gets in the way of the act itself. It is something to do with the concept of 'image'. Everything pretends to be more pretty than it is and the glitz-purveyors pretend to be artists and so involve us in a form of pretending.

Gardeners, at least most of them, are free of this pretension although the catalogues are designed to seduce them with special plastic compost bins and ride-on mowers. Gardeners do not talk about high-level decisions to present the south-west corner as a refreshment-experiencing precinct. They simply take a tea tray out to the flat bit. They do not press delicate fingers to their foreheads and murmur about oriental-influenced conceptualising or refer to a lawn as a pure statement of greenness. They just get on with what needs to be done.

But what *does* need to be done? That's where the judgement varies from gardener to gardener. Some lever themselves out of a Sunday afternoon armchair with a groan to go and mow the grass while others with an equal sense of urgency dig up whole areas of plants and shrubs in order to replace them with different ones closer to the heart's desire. That little piece of land which surrounds one's house is like a canvas to paint on. It requires its owner to be an artist.

It is a sign of what has happened to us that a request to draw something or write a poem will, in most cases, be met by blank refusal. "I couldn't do that." The idea is outrageous. And yet, almost everyone makes a coherent creative statement in the layout and care of a garden. A lot of them are slightly dull and conventional but a surprising number are extraordinarily inventive. Again and again, the eye is delighted by the placing of bright colours against dark and by the grouping of trees and shrubs in a landscape to produce a lovely harmony. It is a true and living art.

Significantly, when a gardener is employed to 'do' the grounds surrounding a large establishment, the result is often as efficient and unimaginative as a parade-ground. "Salvias– wait for it, wait for it – 'shun!" And there they are in their straight rows behind grass verges as short as a sergeant's hair.

It arouses musings on what happens to people when they cease to act on their own judgement but instead do what is thought to be 'proper'. My dream of a truly green society is one in which people live their lives with the care and imaginative energy of gardeners. But then what about the ruthlessness? Oh dear, isn't it difficult. Enough typing for today. I think I'll go and pull up some weeds.

Do birds need prefabs?

4 May 1991

IT IS THE NESTING season. I found half a pale-blue egg shell on the Black Rocks the other day, so I know. Otherwise, since birds are rather private about all that, it would be easy to overlook the whole business until fat little sparrowlings arrive with their harassed parents, shivering their wings as if they are about to die of hunger and opening beaks the size of a miniature JCB bucket. Front loaders, indeed.

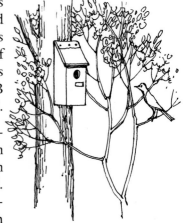

But there's another tell-tale sign. On selected trees in Glen Ashdale square brown nest-boxes have been nailed. They have tough tarpaulin-hinged lids and they are high enough up to prevent enthusiastic visitors from posting empty Irn Bru cans in them, and all they have to do now is attract a house-hunting tit. And I'm trying to work out why I hate them.

It's partly because of the squareness. In a setting where branches slant and cross at narrow angles and everything is intricately patterned, a brown box is obtrusive, as all rectangular things are. A field full of shoebox-shaped caravans is a hideous sight, whereas the Romany caravan has become a treasured folk-museum object. Its roof was curved, its walls slanted, its windows and door and wheels were carved, nothing was straight or square, it was all as detailed as the witch's house of barley-sugar which Hansel and Gretel found so irresistible.

It will be very reasonably argued that the Forestry has more to do with its time than carve nest boxes like cuckoo clocks – and in any case that's only half the story. The other half is about the whole idea that humans have to intervene in a process which has been going on perfectly well ever since the first pterodactyl chirped (or whatever they did). The skeleton of a bird looks amazingly prehistoric. The design has proved itself very effective; it has needed no modification for thousands of years. The nesting system works well because any tit daft enough not to do it properly does not raise young. So birds are presumably as sensible now as they ever were.

Humans, on the other hand, are possessed of a manic conviction that they can improve things. We improved ourselves from cave to cottage to village to town and now live in a state of total dependence on each other. Houses are needed but we cannot put stone on stone and join branch to branch. Instead, factory-made units arrive, or in the latest and most wonderful development, an entire house is shipped in on the back of a lorry. This is indeed an amazing convenience and it might be argued that a widespread scheme of cheap prefabricated building could go a long way towards solving the housing shortage.

But do birds need prefabs? With a million twiggy building-places all over the forest, does the square box serve them any real purpose? The fact is of course that whether the birds need them or not is immaterial.

The nest boxes are there for the purpose of interesting humans rather than birds. We like to feel that we can do anything we've a mind to, so it is vaguely irritating that birds manage to hide themselves from our sight and bring up their families in privacy. The nest boxes are in prominent positions where the public can hardly fail to notice them. They are a tourist attraction.

I don't dispute that the island needs tourists but there is a question to be asked about how far we go towards attracting these human summer migrants and which ones among them constitute a preferred species. It all depends on what they come for. Some, like the rugby-playing hooligans who cannot distinguish enjoyment from depravity, are not welcome, but the majority of our visitors are gentle people who come here for the peace and natural beauty of the place.

Over-management can tame natural beauty and turn it into a park. The island of Rum has suffered this fate with marked nature trails and leaflets. As a result, the people who seek a direct, uninterrupted contact with a natural landscape no loner go there. They still come to Arran. But I regard the nest boxes as just faintly ominous. Prefabs don't belong on trees.

Making your mark

29 June 1991

A VISIT TO LONDON, for the first time in four years or more, can be a dismaying experience. What is this pale blue excrescence they have built on top of Charing Cross station? And where are the cafes and back streets of yesteryear? Swept away in a tide of new building which looks as if it is made of Lotts Bricks, those stone building blocks of childhood, complete with semi-circular arches which, if up-ended and put together, form a circular hole.

The more peripheral parts of London are still as scruffy as ever, if not more so. The great divide between the posh bit and the unposh bit is wider than it used to be. West End underground stations have

Moscow-type murals and mosaics, in contrast to the hell-holes of the outer Northern line. And every train is adorned with the shadowy patterning of graffiti cleaned off but still visible. London Transport posters tell us that it costs two million pounds a year to try and keep the trains clean.

It was a huge relief to come home to Arran, where the tranquil bulk of the hills and the straight line of the horizon seem more fundamental than the shenanigans of human beings. And yet, an uneasiness persists. In the last few weeks, graffiti have spread across the supporting wall of the Glen Ashdale bridge, red and ugly. They speak of a determination to 'make a mark', no matter how crude its expression.

A clued-up Londoner explained that the graffiti there constitute a private code. The symbols and shapes are a language, telling other cognoscenti who drew this, and when, and why. It is the visual equivalent of rhyming slang, an unofficial means of communication, meaningless to the outsiders. Our own little daubers will not know this perhaps, but the style attracts them and so does the hope of having made a permanent statement.

It's nothing new. In the days before the felt-tip and the spray-can, people carried pocket-knives and engraved their initials on school desks, church pews, barrack walls, tree trunks. Even the dubious art of the tattoo is nothing more than self-graffiti, a declaration on one's own skin that Kilroy was here.

Underlying all this is a terrible sense of wasted energy. The London kids will climb over walls topped with barbed wire in order to get at trains standing overnight in yards and they risk death by electrocution to inscribe their mystic messages on bridges and high parts of underground stations. Some have been killed. The need for self-expression, perverted though it may be, is amazingly strong.

It so happens that I've been re-reading William Morris's *News From Nowhere*. Most of our current futurist fiction is pretty grim stuff, envisaging a post-1984 world of thought-police and some form of Big Brother. But Morris had an idyllic view of the society which lay ahead. Everyone would be happy, working for the love of work itself, achieving self-expression in the making of beautiful and useful things. And there would be no money. On the assumption that everyone contributed what they could, all people were valued equally and living was a free process.

In the hundred years since Morris wrote his book, his ideal has come to seem beautiful but naive. Perhaps we have a remnant of it on Arran with our craft-workers and musicians. But in our cities only a mocking ghost survives, in the form of a kid with a spray-can.

77

Trees, incomers and natives

27 July 1991

SOMEWHERE DURING the week I saw a newspaper photograph of a shattered forest. It was the usual kind of thing – tree stumps sticking up pathetically, ground a litter of discarded branches and sawdust. Rainforest, I thought gloomily – but then spotted the caption which claimed that this devastation had been brought about by conservationists in our own country.

The idea apparently, was to create a strictly natural forest of native species only. Not a beech tree was to be left, not a sycamore. So the chain saws moved in.

How long does a tree have to live here before it is a

native? Since the beginning of time it seems. But I'd never seen the beech as a White Settler somehow. With its smooth grey trunk and the spreading beauty of its branches it deserves its old name, The Mother of Forests. Of all trees, its leaf-fall makes the most hospitable of soils in which other species can root and grow.

The sycamore is more obviously an incomer. There is a slightly brash quality about the cheerful way it hurls its little helicopter seed pods about, and the tendency is to regard it as a weed. Its children grow in every cosy place they can find, notably between garden plants and beside drain pipes. I've got one six inches from the back door, getting bigger every minute and it will have to go, otherwise there seems quite a possibility it will knock the house down.

There's a temptation to think of the sycamore as a very large form of Japanese knotweed, that eight-foot monster that seems to need a Sumo wrestler to get it out of the ground. And yet, admiring some turned wooden bowls at a craft fair last year, I was told that they were made of sycamore. The wood was closegrained and silky, a warm pearly grey in colour.

The conventionally approved spruce and larch are valued for their speed of growth, and yet the sycamore is hated for exactly that same speed. In five years a sycamore growing on the bank of the Glen Ashdale burn has grown from being the same size as its neighbouring rowan to tower above it at about three time higher. It lacks the conveniently single-trunked shape of the spruce of course, but its main branches are massive.

I am told that birds will not nest in sycamore. True, the angle at which its limbs branch is wide, perhaps not hospitable to nests. But birds hop about in it quite happily – except for seagulls of course, who prefer chimneys and roofs. The interesting thing is, though, that nobody seems to complain that birds don't nest in Sitka spruce, which is true.

Have we got it wrong? On the one hand there is a blanket prejudice about sycamore despite its obvious good points, and on the other, an insistence on the continued planting of coniferous forest, with all the darkness and loss of undergrowth that this entails. The alternative has always been assumed to be the slow-growing classics of British woodland – the mind turns instantly to the oak with all its symbolism of strength and worthiness. But to fell a mature oak tree is almost more than anyone can bear. By the time it's full grown, it has outlived several generation of humans and become a tradition in its own right.

Old things command respect. We would probably not kill cattle if they had lived since before we were born and gazed upon us with the wisdom of ages. No, we can more easily chop down the quick-grown thing of no particular status. Sycamore for instance, or birch. There's another tough, rapid tree that we could well use. The Scandinavians think birch is great and they know a thing or two about timber.

I despair of the ecologists who will not look and learn from nature itself but go by a book of rules that has been written by somebody with a degree in Earth Science and a head full of romantic notions. Perhaps I am romantic too, remembering the beech woods of childhood and the lovely rustling autumns. But to me, a living museum of native species will never be the same thing.

Talking rubbish?

24 August 1991

WITH ALL THIS speculation about the chosen site for the new coup, the mind rather naturally turns to rubbish. For anyone interested in environmental affairs it's a fairly constant preoccupation at the best of times. Human beings are tremendous rubbish makers.

Animals don't make any rubbish at all. They eat and excrete and the grass grows a little greener as a result. But they possess nothing and so they leave nothing lying about – no crisp packets, no Irn-Bru cans, no broken glass. Their food has no wrappings and their drink comes from the burn or from the dew on the leaves.

Looking at shops cram- med with things wrapped in

other things, it's possible to feel slightly hysterical about the sheer bulk of stuff to be thrown away. Even something as simple as a ballpoint pen tends to be presented for sale in a bulky 'blister pack' with a cardboard backing and a tough plastic front and lots of ecstatic multi-coloured printing in praise of the pen's wondrous qualities. And what do you do with an empty blister pack? You've had to tear the thing to shreds in order to get the pen out anyway but even the most careful approach to opening it leaves you with a totally useless bit of rubbish. It won't hold screws or marbles or photographs or even another pen. It was designed to be thrown away after serving the minimal purpose of making the pen more attractive and more difficult to steal.

We get very used to all this packaging. A bottle of good-for-you pills comes in its own little box and the shop assistant then pops the whole thing into a paper bag. Before getting at the bottle you have to throw away the bag and the box. No wonder the bulk of rubbish to be disposed of is constantly increasing. We are the professional rubbish-makers.

The ecologically virtuous will advise a firm refusal of unnecessary packaging but sometimes this is easier said than done. In a mainland supermarket I once declined the offer of a plastic bag at the check-out, only to be told, "You've got to have it. Management says." On my explaining that it was really not needed, the girl sighed and dropped the bag on the floor at my retreating back. Duty done.

Some countries manage better. A friend from Amsterdam who was here a couple of weeks ago said that every household there had now been provided with a separate bin in which to collect food waste, uncontaminated by plastic or tins. The local authority sent a lorry round to lift this food waste twice a week and it was taken to a separate site where it was composted and eventually sold as high-quality garden manure. It seems a very obvious thing to do. Lumping all the rubbish together in a single hole in the ground is a primitive and wasteful way of going about it. Nothing is retrieved, nothing reused. It costs a lot of money for a process with no end-product whatever.

In the present strapped-for-cash state of Strathclyde, there is no point in advocating a more enlightened approach. Providing bins and going into a programme of public education about rubbish sorting would be immediately expensive and is obviously out of the question. However, rubbish, like charity, starts at home (though I'm not so sure about the charity, come to think of it). Everything that goes down to the coup has first been discarded by someone and pushed into a bin or a black plastic bag. To be strictly logical about the rubbish problem, the place to start must be in the kitchen where a full bin lurks. (Have you noticed how in other people's kitchens, the bin is always full? It seems to be one of those rules of life, in the same way that traffic always arrives when you thought you'd turn the car round in a quiet road.)

Like the coup itself, I've run out of space, having written the week's ration of rubbish. More next time on practical ways of reducing the bulk.

Binhounds

7 September 1991

I HAVE AN ONGOING battle with the more anarchic of my two dogs on the subject of rubbish. I insist that it is to be left strictly alone. She, giving me one of those over-the-shoulder glances, slopes off in the direction of the nearest bin as if obeying some Higher Command. Of indeterminate parentage, she is I suppose a binhound. There are a lot of them about.

You can see her point. It's quite amazing what gets thrown away. Left-over meat pie is prize number one, but half-empty dogfood tins are well worth fishing for and soft biscuits and lumps of margarine. I found her once stripping the wrappings off at least a pound of cheese, slightly mildewed, and there seems to be an endless supply of Mother's Pride. With all these goodies about it's understandable that a dog should try a quick sneak round the corner while I'm hanging the washing out. The seagulls have cottoned on to the same conrnucopia, hurling bits of black plastic about with their great beaks and diving into the rubbish like shoppers at sale time.

Smugly, I reflect on the security of my dustbin with its firmly-fitted black rubber lid. The binhound used to push the lid off at first, so I tied it down with binder twine until she gave up the idea. (The lid, I mean, not the dog; don't start phoning The Cruelty.) But the dreaded black bin bags continue to present an irresistible attraction to all the local dogs and birds, and rubbish gets spread all over the place.

Perhaps it is a lingering effect of a wartime childhood, but I still find all this waste appalling. It seems to be taken for granted that one need not be careful and that buying more than is actually needed is OK. It's certainly OK for those who sell the stuff, like the mustard firm which made a fortune on the yellow dab left on the side of the plate. Waste is profitable.

That of course is the central truth about rubbish. All of it has made money for somebody because it has been bought and discarded. The person who buys no more than his or her actual needs is a dead loss to the commercial system, but such a person doesn't make much rubbish either. Meanwhile, as selling gets more and more successful, there is more and more discarded stuff to be disposed of. Here on Arran it's a big problem.

Without retreating to Buddhist-monk-like existence, there is quite a lot any household can do to reduce the bulk of rubbish. To start with an awful lot of it is air. An empty tin takes up as much space as if it was full. Flattened, it takes up hardly any. If the contents have been taken out with a straight-bladed knife, the tin is relatively clean. Put it on the floor and stand on the open end, then with the other foot stand on the folded-in closed end. Turn it over if necessary and finish it off. There's something oddly satisfactory about this activity. Plastic bottles too, can be stood on. If you screw the cap back on when the bottle is flat, it will stay flat.

The other big reduction is to keep a separate bucket for food waste. Line it with an old newspaper and chuck out the contents onto your compost heap fairly frequently, paper and all, and wash the bucket with hot water before re-use. This habit keeps the dustbin much cleaner because nothing rots in it and from the gardener's point of view, it provides a constant source of good compost. Flat-dwellers can't benefit from this admittedly, but a bit of co-operation between neighbours might provide a compost heap to which several people could contribute.

In the fullness of time, there will be more re-cycling. This is not a crystal ball guess, it's an EC requirement. But re-cycling only works because individual people take the trouble to sort one kind of rubbish from the rest as so many people already do with glass. It'll be interesting to see whether this country ever really takes to it; the Brits cling tenaciously to their right to be careless. Binhounds will have rich pickings for some time yet.

Holy Isle

30 November 1991

A FEW WEEKS AGO A fair-haired girl called Fiona came to lunch. She was doing a research project as part of her course at Glasgow University, trying to find out how Arran people would feel about Buddhists buying Holy Isle.

When a very polite voice on the telephone asked a few weeks later if some Buddhists could come and stay, I'd almost forgotten my absent-minded offer of accommodation. I tend to ask anyone who seems pleasant and agreeable.

So that's how I happened to be on Holy Isle, to my great surprise, with Lama Yeshi and a television crew and some other hangers-on

who were warned sternly to keep out of camera-range and not to talk too loudly. Obeying this instruction, we crept off in the direction of the lighthouse, whispering what a lovely day it was. Even whispers sounded loud. The quiet over there is as deep as a well and Arran by comparison sounds like a noisy beehive, all abuzz with bus engines.

St Molio's cave had graffiti on it. Nothing obscene - just initials, but it was upsetting all the same, specially as there was a very clearly marked 'AP'. Please Miss it wisnae me. I've never been here, Miss, honest. That's one of the troubles about being a Green person - you feel obscurely responsible for the nastiness of the human race. It's bad enough in Glen Ashdale, tutting over the chucked away cans and Marathon wrappers – vandals really do seem to run on peanut power – but on Holy Isle there's a positive sense of desecration.

Lama Yeshi came down the hill in his lemon-yellow wellies and said that something would have to be done to ensure that would-be meditators who came for a people-free retreat were not disturbed. I promptly changed sides and started to worry about all the nature-loving folk on Arran who have felt deprived of a chance to go to Holy Isle all these years, and said so. Lama Yeshi smiled.

Now there is something about Lama Yeshi's smile that is utterly disarming. I had expected to be somewhat in awe of him and that he would have a look-to-the-horizon calm which would seem above all our mundane frettings, but I was completely unprepared for dimples. He smiles with utter infectious happiness and it causes an odd little inward flutter, as if one was very young again and the trunk was being packed to go on holiday.

The next day Holy Isle had retreated into the blowing rain

like a grey shadow of its former self but off they all went again, maroon robes and yellow wellies and cagoules and got thoroughly soaked, chugging round the island in a small boat and landing in unorthodox places and scrambling up hills. Did they still like it? "Oh yes," they said. "Even better." Lama Yeshi had decided that there was room on the island for everyone as long as people respect each other and stay away from areas which are reserved for absolutely uninterrupted tranquillity. It seems reasonable.

Inevitably, the larger newspapers got interested in the story. *The Guardian* carried a facetious piece which made it quite clear that the writer's view of island life was based on a half-forgotten viewing of *Whisky Galore*. The poor soul. There he was, trying hard to be funny in some office in London, while we were being followed along the edge of the sea by a robin that hopped from stone to stone, and the clean water ran chuckling down the hill. There was snow on Arran's peaks and yet the sun shone warmly.

There will be a lot of misunderstanding and a lot of idle curiosity from people who do not understand the bond which can exist between people and the place they live in. To 'fall in love with Arran' means the reason why most people come here and stay here. The Buddhists have fallen in love with Holy Isle and that is the best possible start. Lama Yeshi's smile will do the rest.

Turn of the circle

28 December 1991

THE REASON WHY annual events seem to come round faster and faster, somebody said, is that they form a decreasing percentage of one's total experience. At two years old, another Christmas arrives after half a lifetime, whereas at sixty, it's only the equivalent of one minute in an hour. And if there's anything wrong with the maths, don't tell me. Whatever Christmas is for, it's not nice to spend it standing in the corner wearing a dunce's hat.

What is Christmas for anyway? Spending money, some would say gloomily. Reason seems to be away with the reindeer, abolished by a tide of tinsel and turkey. (Normally moderate column-

ists get carried away by alliteration). It's a funny festival (there we go again), a mixture of ho-ho-ho and Heavenly Host. (This is getting beyond a joke.) I suppose, despite its Christian aspect, it goes back to a much earlier sense of relief that the shortening of the days had stopped and the longer shadow of the standing stone – or of anything else – marked the first sign of the slow climb back to summer.

Despite electricity and the little jumping pictures in a box and all the wonders of the modern world, the length of the days is still there at the back of the mind. For myself, it has more effect on the way I feel than anything connected with shops and the news. Perhaps it has something to do with living here and spending so much time gazing out of the window while pretending to type, but the sky and the sea and the trees seem more real than anything else. When they are not there, something feels wrong. A sense of connectedness is broken.

On these winter days, walking up the glen evokes very strongly the presence of the people who lived here before. Thousands of Christmases ago, long before the Middle Eastern boy in whose name the ancient celebration was hijacked, people made homes somewhere on the hill and came down to the burn for water and saw the drifts of unmelted hailstones lying under the brambles.

Somehow, the spirit of those people lives on. I'm not sure if a hint of them lingers in the stone or in the trees which are the descendents of their trees, or whether their humanity is still ours. Discarding the anxieties about whether the Post Office will manage to deliver the parcels before February and how much booze to buy, one comes down to a desire to be out there with the pattern of bare branches against the sky and the sound of the burn announcing even before one sees it how much water is running over the stones.

There is a new seasonal crop of cards to pin up, another struggle with the gawky emerald green length of flex which doesn't quite reach the Christmas tree and which sheds the little plastic frills off its mini candles. Or there isn't. The circles of time go round and round like the sweep of a radar beam. We'd be in a mess if it stopped.

It's the circling which is the real cause for celebration. One loses sight of it in cities, where trees tend to be crazy Mediterranean things beside artificial fountains in shopping malls. (I'm sure that ought to be spelled 'mauls' judging by the predatory attitude of shoppers.) And the sky is a bit of nothing-much, further up than the top deck of a bus.

On Arran the sky is everywhere, with clouds coming over from the west or more disastrously from the south-east, and it comes right down to the earth. In the case of my house, it comes in through the windows even when shut, and people refer to it unkindly as draughts. But it's usually warmer inside than out, and given time, the summer will come again. Hence the celebration and a thanking of whatever wondrous spirit makes the circle keep turning.

May the new year bring us all its own peace and may we have the sense to enjoy it.

Looking back

25 January 1992

THERE IS A mushroom growing in the back of my car. Well, not an actual mushroom, or it would have been out of there and into the frying pan at once. This is more of a fungus, I suppose. A brown frilly affair sprouting from above the rear wheel arch, revelling in the pure water which drips from the condensation on the tail-gate window.

This particular car seems afflicted with entropy, that natural tendency to return to a pre-organised state. It has clamped both its rear doors shut and will only let me in (with reluctance) to the driver's seat, and its electrical functioning has become occasional. Sometimes things work and sometimes they don't. Driving over the String on a rainy night, it suddenly started switching on its reversing light every time I braked. But have no fear, it doesn't do that any more. There's an eerie glow from inside the engine compartment instead.

Much more of this and there will be a letter from that man in Penrith castigating me for having a car at all - and in truth, if I felt capable of cycling over the String in a howling gale with two dogs and a music stand, I would. The idea of returning to beautiful simplicity is deeply attractive. The photographs of old Arran in a recent *Banner* seemed to be lit with a strange purity and contentment, exuding a fine sense of indifference to the outside world. The place existed within its own dream. When I first came here, at the age of eight, it felt like a different world.

Is it imagination or are places becoming less different from each other? In some ways, the evening-out process is very obvious. There was a time when each town had a flavour entirely of its own but the spread of the dreaded shopping precincts has changed all that. Surrounded by pink neon and Miss Selfridge and the Bradford and Bingley, one could easily become uncertain whether this is Glasgow or Stirling or some other place. To re-establish a connection with the town's essential character, one has to go out of the air-conditioned artificiality and look at something older. In Stirling, a glance across at the hills and the river winding through the narrow strip of flat land at once settles the mind. This is the place which stood – and still stands – at the entry to the Highlands. The castle was built in response to that geography, and the underlying rock is even now more fundamental to the feeling of Stirling than any number of escalators and glass lifts.

In Dublin (so an artist friend tells me, who has an eye for

these things) they insist that all shop fascia boards shall be hand painted. The result, she claimed ecstatically, is that the place has a tremendously individual feel about it, full of its own character. Now, there's a real triumph of human feeling over the forces of commercialism. Back to beautiful simplicity and the skill of doing things by hand.

There's a lot of looking back these days. A high percentage of my Christmas cards this year depicted Victorian children in buttoned boots, with muffs and rosy cheeks and a general air of innocence and chirpiness. Bookshops front their shelves with those old-lace kind of books with pictures of people eating muffins and walking through snow to church. Rennie Mackintosh is newly popular now that he is beginning to seem old fashioned. Nobody is gazing with clear-eyed excitement into the radiant future. I have a sneaking feeling that it was those rampantly optimistic banner-bearing sculptures that finally got the Russians so fed up that they opted for a bit of backward-looking instead.

Richard Jefferies, a Green before his time, wrote a book well over a hundred years ago called *After London*. It's one of those post-disaster epics but full of a naturalist's detailed pleasure in the way the mosses and plants take over the abandoned city, returning it to nature. Jefferies was no believer in progress.

Maybe the fungus growing in my car has moral right on its side. I quite like it being there - as long as it doesn't learn to drive.

These mountains

21 March 1992

GETTING UP FOR THE early boat is less awful now that the days are lengthening. Perhaps I am a slob at heart but it always seems deeply unnatural to get out of a warm bed in pitch darkness. It's funny how electric light can seem warm and cheerful late at night but has a quality of the interrogation cell about it in the morning.

Last week, even though the hail stones were rattling against the window, the daylight was bravely established and the dogs had woken up. On the black mornings they lie there twitching in dream and when woken, look at me with that long-suffering patience accorded to the truly insane. Those torch-lit pre-boat walks are not a lot of fun, but on these lighter mornings they are a pleasure. A crusting of wet snow lies between trees and the cold air pours down the hillside in a fresh torrent and catkins hang on the hazel twigs.

The other day a heron rose from the burn with slow wing-flaps, neck outstretched like a pterodactyl. Birds are weirdly prehistoric if you think of the structure below the coloured feathers – those pointed skulls and wing-bones which might have been hands, but with long feathered fingers that feel the air. Nicer than typewriter keys really. If the Buddhists are right, perhaps next time I'll be a bird. I wouldn't mind.

Driving across to Brodick has its own delights. Having climbed out of Whiting Bay, there is no knowing what awaits the eyes when you reach the Heights. Sometimes there is no sign of the hills at all and everything is swathed in a mist like a Chinese painting. But these recent days have produced a marvellous Alpine scene of white-topped peaks.

Often I think of the words I saw once carved on the long cross-beam of a ski resort café in the French part of Switzerland. Being translated it said, "These mountains, resting in their immense solitude, listen to a truth which humankind cannot hear." Perhaps it is that quality of silent wisdom that brings people to the hills to refresh not just the body with the rhythm of walking but the spirit as well.

There were two young people on the boat last week as it battled its way back from Gourock on a blustery night. They were making their first trip to Arran, asking if Brodick was "near the mountains". When they heard that Goat Fell had been snow-covered the previous day, their eyes lit up like children seeing a Christmas tree. The next moment, a man in a CalMac jacket put his head round the door and said, "Has anybody here lost two wooden toilet seats?" He had a flat package under his arm. There was general merriment over the fish and chips and the young couple glanced at each other and shook their heads. Well, that's Arran for you.

Meeting an Arran friend at Partick underground the other day, we looked at the windy March sky and shrugged. "I really miss Arran in the spring," she said. "It's not the same here." City life takes no great notice of the changing seasons. Rain falls only on tarmac and pavement, not to the roots of bluebells and bramble. In my younger days I used to rush around in the cities enjoying the bustle and the activity. But increasingly now I see it as an artificial construct, every surface human-made and terribly different from things which grow of their own accord.

Natural things are themselves, just as animals and humans are themselves. Blades of grass, pebbles, water and the white peaks of Arran are all themselves, and there is a kind of communication with them. Somehow you can't communicate with tarmac or cement. They do not hear truth as mountains do. Poor things, they don't seem to hear anything at all. And so in cities we don't listen for much. That's why we occupy ourselves with style instead – adverts, designer jeans, designer everything. Thank God no-one can design a mountain.

Slanging match

18 April 1992

"IT'S FUNNY HOW remote this election seems," a friend said as we emerged from the polling station (or 'place' as officialese now austerely has it). We stared across the water at the Ayrshire coast. "It's as if they're having an election and we're allowed to join in," she said.

Well, they've got themselves a government. Outside the window as I write, fine rain drifts and Ayrshire is obliterated. Remoteness is the order of the day. A woman from Ayr once remarked, "Arran comes and goes, you know. We think it's just a cardboard cut-out. Sometimes it's on the horizon and sometimes it's not." She seemed surprised when I told her that was how we felt about the mainland. But then just because a thing is bigger, it isn't necessarily more real. Rather the reverse. It's hugeness which tends to boggle the mind.

This has not been a nice election. There was a time when the hustings brought everyone out in a glow of fervour as brave new worlds were sketched for the entrancement of the voter. Hand-on-heart passion for the righting of wrongs and the stating of rights was an essential characteristic of the candidate, and the person-in-the-street argued fiercely in defence of a vision of a good and true life, made possible by appropriate legislation. The argument was essentially about ideals. But not this time.

We have had a grubby and profoundly depressing slanging match in which no appeal to the voter rose above the nudge-in-the-ribs approach. On both sides, the whisper in the ear was the same – never mind the big issues, which will cost you less, eh? And so we are crudely divided and the parliamentary machine rolls on and the cross on the piece of paper seems curiously meaningless, regardless of which square it went in.

Thus lamenting I went off up the glen with the dogs in search of whatever wisdom could be found from the trees and the burn and the sky. After all, they've been here longer than us and they have seen a lot of silly humans come and go. Clouds hung over the hilltop and the brown water slid quietly over the stones. Chaffinches chased each other about and a good smell of garlic was beginning to come up from the carpet of curved green leaves and knobby buds but my gloom did not lift.

I thought with depression about my conversation with the Scottish Minister for the Environment which might have been so constructive but which revealed such a depth of disconnection between administration and practice. Far from understanding that recycled products need a stable economic 'loop' so that they can command a viable price, the Minister stuck over the definition of cullet as broken glass. "Oh," he said, "yes I suppose some of the bottles do break when people drop them in the thingy."

But then, we do at least have thingies for both clear and coloured glass. . . Progress of a sort is made. But the sense of remoteness remains and with it the feeling that government does not connect with the way we really are. Does it matter? Perhaps not. And yet the feeling that it ought to is hard to suppress.

The dogs, untroubled by such scruples, pottered about on the bank and one of them dug up a stone, sending earth and chunks of rotten wood flying. A rusted beer can dislodged by the digging rolled down the slope and into the water. It floated for a bit then hit a rock and turned over and its triangular hole went under the surface, so it filled up and sank.

Suddenly I laughed. Whatever does it matter? The burn will take its time over dealing with the beer can which will slowly dissolve into the water. Nature is miraculously determined to be its own beautiful self and when we have muddled our way to oblivion the clouds will still blow across the sky and moss will grow on the rotting branches of dead trees and turn them into new soil and the wild garlic will bloom. And the Ayrshire coast will come and go in the drifting rain and herons will see it and buzzards and eagles and gulls. And none of them will bother about whether it's a cardboard cut-out or not.

No messing

2 May 1992

A COUPLE OF evenings ago a heron came and stood in the burn at the bottom of my garden as still as a stone ornament except that the legs, as thin as pea-sticks, had a look of impermanence. Very slowly, the neck extended and the long-beaked head poked forward and the legs bent a little like a cat that crouches to spring, and then the whole thing uncoiled to make a lethal dart at a fish.

Missed. The heron swivelled its head in a See If I Care sort of a way, rather like a shopper who has gone into the Co-op on one of those days when there is more shelf than goods. It took a reproving look at the dog that was barking on the doorstep to be let in, then with immense dignity stepped its way upstream to stand like a pale shadow below the willow tree in the gathering dark.

A few days earlier, a little hawk came to the balcony and sat staring in with a round yellow eye. Yellow claws, yellow hooked beak and a neat round head, the rest of it barred like the midday shadows of corn crossing the palish chest and darker back and long, blunt-ended tail. A kestrel, I supposed. The small birds were absent and silent, but a lot of little eyes were watching. Or so it seemed in that strange moment.

Up the glen the chaffinches have long insistent conversations with each other, repeating complex phrases again and again – a bit like politicians, really. If they go on saying the same thing long enough maybe other people will say it too. But the chaffinches don't and neither do we. The age of the slogan seems to have come to an end. Perhaps there's a natural limit to how much organisation can be tolerated. Nature has its own ideas about that.

Last year, some enthusiastic humans built a dam across the burn and the autumn rain had no way out but to flood round its edges and carry away a lot of the bank together with its bluebell bulbs and sedge and wood anemones. I muttered imprecations and went into yet another state of gloom about the human race. But gradually as the winter went on, the burn dislodged the carefully-placed stones and made gaps for itself then enlarged them, pushing the rocks aside. After one particularly torrential night, it was back to normal, chuckling its way contentedly down its path as it always has done. The swept-away bank is starting to repair itself with washed-up gravel, and grass is rooting.

Entropy, they call it. A tendency to return to an unaltered state. Actually, my dictionary (admittedly rather ancient now) gives some hideously technical definition about how much heat a thing can absorb without getting hot. A bit like keeping one's temper, I suppose. It sounds stressful, but then entropy must be a kind of stress if it results in a definite effort to remain the way one is rather than get heated up. What an interesting idea, though. It sounds as if there is an actual deliberate resistance in natural things to any outside messing about with them. It's a deeply comforting notion.

If nature does have this self-willed quality, it's just as well, because in all the gales of pre-election hot air nobody said a word about the biggest questions of all. Nobody wondered how the poor countries of the world are going to improve the lot of their people without going down the industrial path which is poisoning the planet. Nobody asked how long "the natural resources" can be exploited without doing irremediable damage.

Funny things, people. Specially politicians. I sometimes wonder what we are for. Everything else fits neatly into the scheme of things, but if humans disappeared, nothing would mind much except the odd budgie or tropical fish. Personally, I think that when God rested after all that creative labour and saw that it was good, He created professional witnesses to see that it was good as well. And we are those witnesses.

We seem to have exceeded our brief. Still, it was great fun seeing the heron and the little hawk. All's right with the world – sometimes.

The smell of the garlic

16 May 1992

OF ALL THE THRILLS that can be bought from shops and travel agents, there is nothing to equal waking up to find the sun shining. After weeks of welly-booted mornings which offer only the mild triumph of not getting actually soaked, the glow of light across the bedroom ceiling is a joy.

The dogs know it too. Panting cheerfully, they come and suggest that it's time we were up and out. One of them helpfully brings me a sock. They're quite right – it's nice to be away up the glen before other people have the same idea. Nodding and smiling at thirty cagoule-clad hikers is a big interruption to the thought-processes and what's more – I hate to be indelicate about this – they leave a waft of after-shave and deodorant behind them which conflicts oddly with the smells of the woodland.

It might be worse, I suppose. I am the idiot who sat down next to a bag-lady on the Glasgow underground and realised with watering eyes exactly why it was that everyone else had moved away. But at this time of the year, half the delight of being out on the hill is the scent of it. There is always the background of damp earth and tree-bark but in May the drifts of wild garlic give off a heady aroma as vibrant as the Hallelujah Chorus. On a sunny morning when the light beats down through the beech twigs and the young leaves shine as sharply as the taste of green apples, it's enough to dizzy the brain with happiness.

On top of all that, bluebells are unrolling themselves, spreading their haze of colour under the trees and adding their own sweetness to the scent of the garlic. The bracken is having a second shot at unrolling, having had a nasty setback last month when the cold wind blasted it brown. It was so shocked that it just stood there hugging itself like someone whose clothes have been blown off. But it's feeling better now and is behaving in its usual brash way, preparing to march all over the soft emerald grass which grows in the strange circular patch just up from the old sheep-dip. Is it imagination or does bracken too have a faint scent a little like cloves, spicy and yet musky? It's a dry, rustling smell which looks ahead to the hot brownness of October, even when the fronds are new and green.

As mere humans, we are shut out from a whole world of exciting and significant smells. There are always the mysterious pheronomes, the ultras-sonics of the olfactory world, which do things to us quite undetected by our dull old noses, but it would be much more fun to know what's going on. Dogs have a lovely time sniffing the wind and knowing what is happening out there just by the little wafts of scent that come to them. And it's no use thinking they can be put off the scent (as you might say) by chemical means. I once used a spray which reeked of lemon peel to try and kid the local dogs that my bitch was not in season. Within five minutes notwithstanding the spray (or notwithwrigglingunderthegate, to be more accurate), they had identified the disguise and contemptuously discarded it.

Progress does not approve of smells. The argument seems to be that it's better to have no smells at all than to risk encountering a nasty one, so everything becomes blander and more sanitised. Rooms without windows are more and more common – not just bathrooms with those noisy fans that are switched on with the light, but lecture theatres. Not even a skylight. That'll stop their mental truancy – no gazing out of the window here.

There is even the windowless office. *The Guardian* computer page last week contained a bizarre piece about an electronically hypersensitive desk which, through sensors and mikes and cameras, interpreted and acted on every casual tap of your pen. "You do not have to take your eyes off the desktop," the piece claimed ecstatically.

What, no gazing out over the beach? No tapping of the pen which means nothing at all? Such efficiency is my idea of hell on earth. The inventors are clearly insane and should be gently led on daily walks to smell the wild garlic and be glad they are alive.

Getting battier?

5 September 1992

PEOPLE SEEM TO BE getting battier. I read the other day about a proposed orchestral play-in, a kind of ordeal by Vivaldi which would go on for 24 hours. The players presumably would take over from each other in relays, handing over flutes like batons (how difficult to do it discreetly with a 'cello), but the conductor intended to keep going by means of an intravenous drip plumbed in up the sleeve of his penguin suit. I don't know why he couldn't just have a bottle of glucose drink clipped to his music stand with a long straw, like a Milk Race cyclist but perhaps it wouldn't have the same charisma. The audience would probably pay the

money simply in the macabre hope that the needle would come unstuck.

And what was it all for? To raise money for something or other, no doubt. The do-gooders get ever more desperate as the do-badders collar all the cash. They ring you up these days, asking in nice warm personal voices if you will commit yourself to £10 a month for ever. You can understand why. Most of the money in the world goes round and round in circles, being passed from hand to hand in a hideously important game. The players, like all players, are madly keen on it, scanning papers for news on the state of play with all the fanaticism of cricketers in search of the latest test score.

Nowadays you are either a player in this game or you are not. Me, I'm a non-player. The things I really like are quite impossible to buy, so there's no point in spending a lot of energy in doing things I don't like for the sake of making money. This is not, as someone famously said, a dress-rehearsal – this is it. There's nothing quite so magical as Now, in the moment of gazing at that straight grey horizon or seeing how the trees in the forest hold out green hands to the light.

I suspects that this delight in the free unprofitable beauty which lies all around us is becoming subversive. The papers solemnly report the government's dismay at the failure of the public to get itself into debt for the sake of constructing 'a buoyant economy', and gazers at leaves are the last people to be enthusiastic about that particular game.

Even medicine is starting to detach itself from the financial gallop to some extent. Someone declared last week that it is now scientifically proved that stroking domestic animals is good for you. It lowers blood pressure and makes you much less vulnerable to heart attacks. Lousy news for Ciba-Geigy and other chemical giants, but very smug-making for those of us who like to curl up with a cat. Perhaps this is why officialdom disapproves so strenuously of all things 'alternative'. It's not the fear that you may get hemlock mixed in with your comfrey and die a nasty Socratic death that makes them mutter about hippiedom, but a suspicion that you are not going to troop into Boots and buy whatever ICI has decreed to be appropriate. Non-buying has become the present-day sin.

The big dilemma is how to steer a path between playing and non-playing the money game. A letter this week reminded me that some people have a foot in both camps and struggle to find a way of balancing the interests of enterprise with a concern for things natural. This long and very interesting letter was from Kerr Robertson, outlining plans for the eventual clearing and improving of the Giants' Graves site once the standing timber matures, and explaining the problems of finding a good, non-crunchy material for the surfacing of the paths.

It must be extraordinarily difficult to grow a profitable crop of timber and at the same time cater for the grumbling children of nature like myself who yearn for unspoilt wilderness, and Kerr Robertson (seriously, now) has my greatest admiration for the way he manages it. The opening up of the Iron Age Fort and the re-establishing of Loch Ime have been marvellous additions to the interest of walking on Arran's hillsides. If people are really getting battier, it must be only over there in the great Wild Wood of the mainland.

Ireland

17 April 1993

HOW IS IT, I WONDER, that atmosphere can make itself felt, even through the windows of a bus? Staring out at the place through which you are travelling, the flavour is oddly evident though diluted. Having hurtled round the south-west of Ireland with occasional escapes from the mobile glass box to poke about and explore, I came back to Arran with a whole lot of entirely unexpected impressions of that place which we can see (on a good day) as a blue line beyond Kintyre.

Some of the conventional ideas about Ireland turned out to be true – it really is as green as they say, and as slow-moving and relaxed and funny and the Guinness a

111

tone-poem of creamy bitterness. What I hadn't realised was the complete absence of the chainstores that make Scottish towns look increasingly like English ones and stamp their sameness over every shopping centre. In Ireland every shop is an individual one, every pub a Free House known by its owner's name. This lively variety is one of the things that makes for the cheerful, independent atmosphere of the place.

Another thing is the youthfulness of the population. It turns out that over half of Ireland's young people are under 25 years old. Young people are about everywhere in amiable groups, talking and laughing and remarkably untruculent, and this adds to the feeling that Ireland is confident and optimistic, charged with a sense of its own value, amused by its own wit. Despite the laid-back attitude to time, there is a latent excitement that produces an odd 'buzz'. The place seems happy.

This is not to say of course that people do not have their personal ups and downs, but the overall feeling is astonishingly lighthearted. The colours help to convey this impression. Houses are painted with a cheerful abandon which is almost Mediterranean, pink and orange, cobalt and red and turquoise, all the shades clear and glowing.

And yet, the ruins of older houses stand in the fields as a stark reminder of what happened to Ireland only a century ago when the people died of starvation as the English landlords took their cattle and sheep in lieu of the rent they could not pay. It was not from choice that potatoes were the only food available and that there was no other resource when the blight destroyed that fragile life-line.

Reading Liam O'Flaherty's *Famine* on the bus was perhaps a mistake, for it is a book which arouses a shaking passion of pity and anger. But it is a necessary understanding, laying bare the reasons why Ireland had to establish its own identity as an independent nation. Those reasons live on and it is not for nothing that every folk music session in a pub ends with the standing-up of every person present for the playing of the National Anthem. It made me sad for Scotland.

Coming back through the outskirts of Belfast to Larne was a very different experience. No clear colours and gaiety there, only a harsh greyness, with frightened young soldiers standing in the streets and the bus brought to a halt again and again by the queues of traffic waiting to get through the road blocks. On a big road-sign at a roundabout, the exit to Falls had the spray-canned alternative title lettered beneath it – Provoland. It was a stale, sour atmosphere which made its way through the bus windows and almost everyone muttered about the advantages of flying or using alternative routes to the Republic so as to avoid going through Belfast again.

And coming home? As always, it was a pleasure. Arran is its own place with its own happiness very different from mainland Scotland. At a cheerfully batty Saturday night session in a Whiting Bay pub, there was some good music played and some inspired solo dancing. There's nothing like living in one of the most beautiful places on earth; it brings its own confidence. I wonder if it filters through the bus windows to touch tourists who come here and stare out, trying to understand. I hope so.

Glow of gold

7 August 1993

HOLIDAYS. NOW there's an evocative word. For me, it conjures up the curiously spicy smell of the cabin trunk which when I was very young used to be packed and sent on ahead of us. It was lined with mauve and white ticking and to this day the sight of those particular narrow stripes is enough to set me in a flutter. The smell – I realise now – was a waft of India left from my grandmother's days in the Raj. But oh, the excitement!

We're so matter of fact about it these days. Airports are deliberately downbeat. They whisk away all signs of luggage, sooth you with tubular steel armchairs, and television screens do all they can to minimise the shocking

fact that you are about to be hurled into the air in a winged bullet to land in a place where the sun is on the other side of the sky. Flying is too much for the mind to grasp; one is not so much a traveller as a studier of meals on plastic trays, a loo-queuer, a gazer at overhead signs. Flying is anti-romantic.

Small planes are much funnier and more alarming, buffeted about in the air currents, climbing over hills like little airhorses, landing on beaches and in fields. On a clear day when you can see down they give you a real feeling of going somewhere. They never, thank goodness, quite manage to achieve the time-capsule effect. But for the real salty thrill of genuine travelling, give me boats every time.

Just listen to this, on a postcard from last weekend's visitor – "As we sailed away, the clouds parted and the sun speckled the sea and the island with light. I am just full of it and am wandering around work with a glow of gold feeling of a time so happily spent." And he only comes from Glasgow. That's the essence of the holiday feeling, a magic interlude which lives on afterwards.

For Arran residents it's terribly easy to get settled into the day to day business of making a living and lose sight of the way that visitors see the place. Why do they come here instead of taking the effortless time-capsule route to resorts with guaranteed sunshine and cheap wine? It's an important question 'specially for those who have a financial interest in providing holidays. You need to know what it is about Arran that people like.

I know what my visitors like, because they join me in my own enjoyment in the beauty of the place and the quiet and the odd refreshing sense of having come to an island which is its own self, separate and different from the mainland, continuing its own life which has gone on for thousands of years. The old stones of prehistory are casually intermingled with our current use of the hills, and it does not require much imagination to see with the eyes of those who lived here with nothing but their skill and infinitely detailed knowledge of these natural surroundings.

Things can happen here which would never occur in Benidorm. Out the other night with the dogs at midnight, a bat was tumbling to and fro in the air, swooping low as if to inspect us, and a hedgehog was pattering about on its neat little feet, doing a good job with the slugs – and, strangest of all, there was a wild, croaking cry from the beach as a heron flapped slowly up, pale in the darkness.

Some people don't want all that. A sea-shore blazing with light and richly smelling of chips and vinegar and candyfloss has its own delights. But it's no use looking there for the primal magic of a place which is still its own self. Such ancient places are becoming rare, for the creeping erosion which masquerades as progress nibbles away at them with lights and pavements and bigger buses, and the magic folds its wings and creeps away to its secret retreats in the hills where it may be glimpsed, if at all, only through binoculars from the permitted tourist paths. The goose which lays the 'glow of gold' egg is a rare and precious bird. We must guard her carefully.

Hedgehog

4 September 1993

I NEVER KNEW UNTIL this week how adept hedgehogs are with their hands. Late-ish one night, Annie the poodle went into a hysterical performance of trying to fire herself through the catflap like a cork out of a pop-gun. And the cause of the fandango was a hedgehog, calmly finishing off Charlie's saucer of milk outside the back door.

As the milk went down, a small dark hand was extended from under the prickles to take the saucer by its edge and tip it to bring the little pool nearer to the surprisingly pink tongue. Out of curiosity I offered the visitor the remains of Charlie's Choosy which was going a bit dry on its saucer. Before you could say, "Slug", it was being

wolfed (or hedgehogged) down – but that's where the real handiness came in. The natty black fingers scooped the stuff in like someone wiping an eggy plate with a bit of bread, and within a couple of minutes the saucer was clean. Mrs Tiggywinkle toddled off as pleased as a Glasgow housewife after a good shopping haul in Every's. A right happy wee hedgehen? No, this is getting ridiculous.

It's such a great time of the year, this awakening out of the August stillness. The birds are released from all that dreaded breeding, with its constant pushing of grubs down gobs, and have started to sing again, even though the twitters and chirps are staccato now, very different from the romantic trilling of spring. With the days shortening towards winter, there's a brisk dusting of hands, jobs done. Right, that's you brought up son, away you go.

Leaves are detaching themselves from the trees, even when there is no wind, spiralling gently down to land on the earth or go sailing down the burn, lodging against stones, making little yellow islands. The tree has separated itself from them, sealed off the sap-flow, returned to its own self with next year's buds contained in embryo form, held safe against the cold.

And the great slow beech still has this vast family of complex seeds about her, even though she is six inches bigger in every direction than she was last year, and broader and deeper rooted. If as the Buddhists say, we are born again and again in different forms, I'm putting in a request to be a beech tree. I like the idea of that rootedness. Relieved of all the rushing about, maybe one could get down to a bit of serious meditation.

But there again, the use of one's legs is a great boon. How

else would I get to see marvellous sights like the little red lamps of wild fuchsia which seem to glow in a surrounding darkness even at midday? And there was moss growing on a smooth grey sycamore tree, minuscule fingers of it creeping out, astonishingly detailed, like microscopic fir branches, though at the same time you could see it as a Boeing eye view of a rainforest.

There must be some reason why so many people feel the urge to get away from all the business of life and go wandering through woods and across hills. Tucked away in our ancestry is an ancient need to be in touch with the bark of beech trees and the ever-running water of the burn. And meanwhile a large slug has felt the urge to come into my kitchen and climb up the wall. Serves me right. I've probably turned the resident hedgehog into a junk food addict.

Run for your life

18 September 1993

HOW LOVELY THEY were, those days of Indian summer which have now given way to a blustery Scottish autumn. For a blissful couple of weeks there were clear blue skies, and the air was warm enough for a discarding of cardigans and a turning of the face to the sun like a grateful chrysanthemum. The daft doings of humans receded to the level of a dull nagging, easily forgotten, but now the white-edged waves come crawling in over the stones and the wind buffets the thinning leaves, and with a sigh I turn to letters.

I think moderation taken to excess is immoderate. Faced with a plan to change the village in which I live, neutrality is impossible. You either think the changes are good or you don't. And shrugging indifference is not neutrality, it's a cop-out. For myself, after a lot of poring over plans and gazing at drawings of posts and chains there can be no indifference.

We've seen things like this before. Walk from the boat to the train at Ardrossan and note the municipal bed of shrubs and crisps bags edging the diagonal brick path. Dead modern. Have a look at Stevenston where all edges are 'defined' by kerbs and there's no shortage of posts and chains. Attractive? Relaxed? Full of rural charm which makes you want to spend two weeks' holiday there? Well, hardly.

Real improvements have to make people feel better about the place they live in. The secure carpark at Ardrossan was a real improvement, bringing peace of mind which was certainly not there before. The straight drive-through onto the boat made life easier and such things as the new bigger postbox in Whiting Bay are genuinely helpful because the little box simply couldn't manage all the mail. And the new boat is comfortable. But the tarting-up approach has nothing to do with real improvement. It's like offering cosmetic surgery instead of dentistry – just plain silly.

I'm inclined to agree with Thoreau who said, "If I knew for a certainty that a man was coming to my house with the conscious design to do me good, I should run for my life."

Children too, have a healthy instinct to resist being done good to. In the name of improvement they have to submit at the very least to the small indignity of no longer being able to choose their own preferences. They are called in from play, inspected, tutted over, washed, made presentable and cautioned not to go out and get mucky again. And they very sensibly resent it.

Ah, planners, do you not realise that the dearest wish of humans is to play? Given our hearts' desire, we amble, we potter, we eat messy ice-creams and go for muddy walks and sit about in old clothes in the sunshine. We go to untidy islands and dabble in burns for fish and hit little white balls about on odd-shaped tracts of grass or lounge beside the car looking at seagulls. If the Tourist Board had any sense, it would be putting its collective brains together in an effort to understand just what is the appeal of Arran and why it is that people come here. Instead, it seems hell-bent on the setting up of a mechanism for the efficient handling of the maximum numbers. The design of a slaughter-house works on exactly the same principle; the system is slick but the views of the individuals passing through are not, shall we say, paramount.

It seems to me that we are in the grip of a strange new disease of the mind, failure of the immune system to be immune to systems. We seem incapable of defending ourselves against silly ideas once they have developed into the money and plans stage. Thus – can you believe this? – the excuse given for continuing this unpopular plan is that a lot of money has already been spent on it. In other words, the planners like their plan and the people planned for have no more reality than those ghostly figures sketched in by draughtsmen as adjuncts to plastic bus-shelters and arty triangular spaces beside the carparks. And posts and chains. The system is devouring us. But I'm kicking all the way down.

Benidorm adrift

31 December 1993

IT IS STRANGELY QUIET on these mornings of deep frost, as if the very air is clamped into a coldness that will not convey sound. The birds flit silently to their nut-feeders on the balcony and the frozen path through the forest does not crunch under-foot. Only the indomitable robins flit through the bushes pip-pipping hopefully, knowing there are currants in my pocket.

The days dwindle down as the Kurt Weill song says. When else could a New Year start? It's not one of those theoretical things like when you start your Income Tax year. It's the real aboriginal feeling that we have stopped dwindling and have started to grow again.

MV WHITE ELEPHANT

123

I don't know if we get older and wiser – I can think of one or two Elder Statespersons who seem to get sillier by the day – but speaking for myself, I get less patient with things that aren't real.

Take the new boat for instance. The Calamity Isles is pure *Brigadoon* – now you see me, now you don't. Am I at Gourock? Am I skulking at Brodick? But never mind what it does. I'm concerned with what it is and why it came to be that way.

How is it that a Scottish island on a stretch of water with a narrowish pier at one side and a windswept constricted harbour entry at the other ends up with a faery (no, that's the typewriter doing a Feudian slip), a ferry which looks like a bit of Benidorm that's somehow come adrift? A tall white floating hotel with a huge car park in it is not the real working boat that the island needs.

Yes, it is plusher. And yes, it theoretically turns on a sixpence. But sixpences are in short supply in the Clyde in mid-winter and the theory somehow never marries up with what it's really like to live on Arran and need to travel to and fro.

One can only assume that the theory did not concern itself with that particular reality. Otherwise we'd have had what most people wanted – two smaller boats, one of which could come off the run in the winter and double as a stand-by boat to cover the periods of annual refit or of particularly heavy demand. Ah, but think of the crew cost, they will say. (At least, I expect they will. But you never know because they don't actually say anything.) What, we ask with a delicate cough, about the cost of the Charismatic Isles?

Here we enter cloud-cuckoo land. It is said that government money was available only to provide a new vessel for the profit-making run. (Bad luck, Stornoway. You'll just have to go on sitting on your suitcases.) It is said that the boat was designed for carrying the maximum number of vehicles. Well, we can see that – otherwise we wouldn't have to climb into it through the bedroom window.

Much else is said. Rumours fly and there is no way of proving them true or untrue. The Collapsible Isles has a draught of only ten feet – some say eight feet – so it can't be sailed in the Minch or the Irish Sea. The steering engines can't compete with the wind-thrust on the high freeboard. As we teeter to and fro to Gourock, wrangling over the question of where to put our dogs, forbidden on its expensive carpets, the unanswered questions nag. Why does CalMac not communicate with the people for whom this boat, or any boat, should provide a service? Anyone would think they would go on playing at ferrybiz even if Arran suddenly did an Atlantis and disappeared under the waves. Island? What island? Oh, never mind, how are the figures looking?

It all comes back to a question of how people feel. Once this is ignored, the theories will not connect with the reality of travelling. Our problem for 1994 is how to communicate the way we feel to the mad magicians of the accounts departments and the drawing boards. The government supports the idea of a Citizen's Charter. Great. It is time it applied it to CalMac.

A happy New Year to you all.

For a full list of titles
available from
Argyll Publishing,
send S.A.E. to:–

Argyll Publishing
Glendaruel,
Argyll
PA22 3AE